Going for Self Employment

Moulton College

NORTHAMPTONSHIRE

Profit through Skill

If you want to know how. . .

Starting Your Own Business
How to plan and build a successful enterprise

Your Own Business
The complete guide to succeeding with a small business

Book-keeping & Accounts for the Small Business
How to keep the books and maintain financial control over your business

Preparing a Winning Business Plan
How to create a plan that gains investment and gives direction

Send for a free copy of the latest catalogue to:
HowTo Books
3 Newtec Place, Magdalen Road,
Oxford OX4 1RE, United Kingdom
email: info@howtobooks.co.uk
http://www.howtobooks.co.uk

Going for Self-employment

How to set up and run
your own business

Second edition

JOHN WHITELEY

howtobooks

Originally published as *Be Your Own Boss*

Published by How To Books Ltd, 3 Newtec Place,
Magdalen Road, Oxford OX4 1RE. United Kingdom.
Tel: (01865) 793806. Fax: (01865) 248780.
email: info@howtobooks.co.uk
http://www.howtobooks.co.uk

First published 2002
Second edition 2004

British Library Cataloguing in Publication Data
A catalogue record for this book is available from the British
Library.

Cartoons by Mike Flanagan

Produced for How To Books by Deer Park Productions
Typeset by PDQ Typesetting, Stoke-on-Trent, Staffs.
Cover design by Baseline Arts Ltd, Oxford
Printed and bound by The Cromwell Press, Trowbridge,
Wiltshire

NOTE: The material contained in this book is set out in good
faith for general guidance and no liability can be accepted for
loss or expense incurred as a result of relying in particular
circumstances on statements made in the book. Laws and
regulations are complex and liable to change, and readers should
check the current position with the relevant authorities before
making personal arrangements.

Contents

Preface

Working for yourself – is it a paradise world? Do you escape the tyranny of working for a boss who is unsympathetic? Or is it a drudge, weighed down by regulations and paperwork?

Many people would perhaps like to be self-employed, but have never experienced life outside of a nine-to-five job. By the end of reading this book, you should have some idea of what the world of the self-employed is like.

It can be a frustrating world, when your plans are upset by unforeseen circumstances. It can have its boring times, when the work is hard and monotonous. It can be mentally tough, when the temptation to down tools and relax battles against your self-discipline. But it can be rewarding, both in terms of financial return, and in terms of the satisfaction of achievement.

Over and above all this, however, being self-employed means that you are in control. Your destiny is in your own hands. No matter how many unforeseen circumstances arise, or seemingly impenetrable obstacles crop up, the answer lies with you alone. If the idea of taking responsibility for your own decisions frightens you, you must overcome that fear, or perhaps give up the idea of being self-employed.

Being self-employed may not be for everybody; it takes a special sort of person to succeed. Simply reading this book does not guarantee that you will succeed – although

I hope it will help you. In the end, only you can provide the will to succeed, and the ability to carry it through.

If you have read this far, my message now is – have confidence in yourself, and go for it!

John Whiteley

List of Illustrations

Taking the Decision

ANALYSING YOUR MOTIVES

Why do you want to become self-employed? This is the first and most basic question to ask yourself. You may think it is not worth giving time to answering the question, but I want to challenge you. Answer the question – not just mentally, but write down your answer. Writing down your answer helps you to organise your thoughts.

Giving this question some thought may lead you to come up with more than one answer. Your reasons may be a complex of interweaving factors.

Here are some possible answers – were any of these in your list?

- I have been made redundant. I have always wanted to run a pub, and someone suggested that I could use my redundancy money for something like this.

- I have this really good idea for a completely new product (or process, or service) and I think it could be successful. I want the chance to back my judgement.

- I am fed up with the nine-to-five daily grind. I want the freedom of working for myself, so I can take a day off if I feel like it, without my boss bitching about it.

ELIMINATING THE NEGATIVE ASPECTS

When you have written down all your motives for wanting to be self-employed, try to work out which are the negative aspects, and which are the positive aspects.

> **Work on the negatives.**

This does not mean denying their validity in any way – you must be honest with yourself about this process. You do not have to justify these reasons to anyone else. Trying to evade the issue or fudge any explanations will only affect yourself.

What this *does* mean is evaluating how strong the negative factors really are. Quite frankly, being self-employed is not all beer and skittles. It takes determination, perseverance and self-discipline. If the only reasons, or the main reasons, for wanting to be self-employed are negative ones, then you must think seriously about whether you go any further down this road. Negative reasons will not be adequate to keep you going through the tedious parts, and the sheer hard work.

BUILDING ON THE POSITIVE ASPECTS

Next, look at the positive aspects. Even if your first thoughts showed up more negative aspects, there must be some positive aspects. A second, deeper contemplation may well bring to light some positive aspects you never suspected were there.

Whatever positive aspects you find, try to build on them. Think about them and see how you can develop them.

One of the most important ways of succeeding is to play to your strengths. Thinking about your motives will reveal your own strengths to you. These will be the qualities you will use in the course of your working life as your own boss.

THINKING MORE DEEPLY

So far, if you have followed my advice, you will not have actually *done* anything except think. This is important, because becoming self-employed is a big step to take. It will affect your whole life – not just your working life. Your social life may have to change, and you must think seriously about the effect on your family life.

In fact, it will affect other people's lives as well. Talk to your wife, husband or life partner about this decision. If you have children, talk to them about it. Becoming self-employed may mean that the amount of time you have for your family will be affected. It may mean that other members of your family – wife, husband, parents, brothers or sisters – can actually be involved with you in your new venture.

Certainly you will need the support of your family throughout – and particularly as you start out. They will have to understand that you will become immersed in the new business, and they may be sucked in as well. In the early years particularly, their standard of living may suffer.

CHECKLIST

1. Analyse your motives.
2. Write them down.

3. Eliminate the negatives.

4. Build on the positives.

5. Think, and discuss your plans with those around you.

CASE STUDIES

Melanie is given an opportunity

Melanie is in her early twenties and is a hairdresser. She has been working for Doreen in a salon. Doreen takes her aside and tells her that she is going to have to give up the salon, as her husband has been offered a promotion which means moving away. Doreen offers Melanie the chance to take over the salon, saying that she is offering it to her before the other girls in the salon, because she thinks that Melanie is the one who works best with the customers, and has the best chance of making a go of it.

Melanie has never considered before the possibility of working for herself, and at first she is frightened of the idea. But she promises to think about it and tell Doreen her answer in a week. She talks to her parents, her boyfriend and her best friend from school.

As she thinks about it, she becomes more enthusiastic. She thinks about the ways in which she might improve the salon's appearance, and possibly expand if the premises next door become available. There is also the prospect of diversifying by starting manicure and other beauty treatments. She finally tells Doreen that she will give it a go, and suggests a date to talk about what Doreen is expecting to be paid for the business.

POINTS TO CONSIDER

1. How enthusiastic are you about wanting to be self-employed?

2. What first prompted you to think about becoming self-employed?

3. Have you done anything about your desire?

4. Is there any factor which has been stopping you going further until now?

(2)

Adjusting Your Mindset

Once you take the step and become self-employed, you enter a new world. The change may take a little while to adjust to, but if you address the issues actively, the adjustment becomes easier.

BUILDING SELF-DISCIPLINE

Self-discipline is one of the key essentials in being self-employed. You have nobody to answer to except yourself. Self-discipline comes more easily to some people than others, but for everybody, the change from being employed (or unemployed) to being self-employed involves a greater exercise of self-discipline.

Most people find that when they work for themselves, they are working for the hardest, most ruthless boss they have ever had!

Setting goals and targets

Setting achievement targets, not task targets
One of the most effective ways of building self-discipline is to set yourself goals and targets, related to achievements rather than tasks. If you were to try to exercise self-discipline by saying, for example, 'I must work 35 hours in the shop this week, and 5 hours doing the paperwork', that is easily subverted or upset by unexpected interruptions. The target is task-related.

If you set achievement targets, the detail of the tasks involved does not need so much attention to self-regulation. So, you may set yourself a goal of, say, increasing the shop sales of 5% over last month. That sort of target motivates you to think about ways in which you could increase the sales.

Sorting out the wheat from the chaff

Setting yourself achievement targets helps you to concentrate on the things that are important, and this in turn helps your self-discipline.

> **Remember – the most urgent things are not necessarily the most important things.**

Keeping it going

The process of setting targets and monitoring performance is one which continues throughout your career as a self-employed person. It affects all areas of your business life. The details of this process are considered in more depth in Chapter 4. Part of the self-discipline you need is to keep up this process of planning, setting targets, monitoring progress, and if necessary amending your targets. This applies to the main areas of your business – in particular to sales, costs and capital expenditure.

> **Do not be tempted to coast along without carrying out this process. It is vital.**

Doing the boring bits

However much you concentrate on the important things,

there are inevitably going to be the many routine, tedious jobs, which are mostly of an administrative nature. You are just going to have to grit your teeth and get on with them (unless you are one of those rare people who actually enjoy this work and look forward to it).

SETTING YOUR OWN WORKING HOURS AND HOLIDAYS

Part of the fun of working for yourself is not having a boss to answer to – except yourself. However, you may find it useful to set out for yourself a working week, and try to arrange your holidays in advance, then book them in your diary. Depending on the nature of your work, many things have to be arranged some time in advance. If you have an outline of your normal working hours, and holiday days, then you can plan ahead to get cover if needed for the holidays, and plan how to fit into your working week the things that need to be done.

Once you are in a framework like this, you will find that you are able to take the occasional unplanned day off – so long as it does not happen too often!

PLAYING TO YOUR STRENGTHS

When you start to work for yourself, you will soon find out that you have to learn many new skills. Later on, if the business expands, you may have to get other people to do some of those things. To start with, however, you may have to do them all yourself. In fact, it is good to have hands-on experience of all the little jobs which need to be done, even if you get someone else to do them later.

Right from the start, however, learn to play to your own strengths. As you start learning new skills, you will find that there are some things you do well, and others you are not so good at. Concentrate on the things you do well. You may find, for example, that you are a good salesperson. If so, concentrate on selling and marketing your product or service. If you are better at designing, or producing the product, then concentrate on that.

However, do not get tempted to take it too easy. A key element of self-discipline is to learn when you are slipping into the 'comfort zone'. This occurs when you want to keep things too easy and comfortable. To be successful, always try to pitch your level of achievement just beyond that comfort zone, so that you always have something to strive towards.

> **Remember – the things you like doing**
> **are generally the things you do best.**

PUTTING THE CUSTOMER FIRST

When you work for yourself, you no longer receive a regular pay packet every week or month. It is up to you to earn your keep. That means you have to induce your customers (or clients) to provide your pay packet.

The only way to do that is to provide them with a product or service they are willing to pay for. Therefore, all your efforts must serve that end – satisfying the customer. If you are developing new products or services, they are only of use if the customers perceive them as something they want – and are willing to pay for. If you are selling, you have to convince the customer that:

- They want this product or service.
- They want yours rather than anyone else's.
- They want more of it.
- They are willing to pay your price – or at least willing to negotiate a price.

If you are producing the goods, you must be sure that they meet the customer's specification, and that they are of good enough quality.

If you are delivering services, make sure that you always beat your promise and the customer's expectation. In the case of services, the timing is always important. Make sure that your promised delivery date is achievable. It is then a good tactic to add on a day or two, so that you can be sure of beating the date deadline.

Example

John and Jack are delivering the same service – industrial cleaning. They both have the same job to do. John promises he will have the job done by Tuesday. Jack promises he will have the job done by Thursday.

They both start on the same day – Monday – and finish the job on the same day – Wednesday. Jack's customer will be more satisfied because he has had the job finished earlier than he expected. John's customer will be disappointed because he will see the job finished late. Yet they both took the same time to do the job!

Remember – perception is everything.
What matters is not how long you took or how well you actually did the job, but how the customer perceived it.

Another important thing to bear in mind about providing a service is that your customers will only want to buy your services if they can see that your services really provide them with something of value. So try to promote your services as 'added value' services. Convince the customers that you can really add value to their business or product, rather than simply complying with regulations (like filling in a tax return). They will then be much more willing to use your services in the future.

So keep repeating to yourself, 'The customer is king', like a mantra. Whatever area of your job you are doing, think about it from your customer's point of view – how does it contribute to meeting the customer's needs?

Sell yourself

Always remember that you are not just selling a product or service. You are selling yourself. Your customers will not just make judgements about your product or service – they will make judgements about you. You must demonstrate that you give the quality of service a high priority. Make sure that the first order for a customer is not the last, but the start of a new business relationship.

Remember who pays for you to make a living.

CHECKLIST

1. Build up your self-discipline.

2. Set yourself achievement goals and targets.

3. Sort out what is important.

4. Set your own agenda and working pattern.

5. Find out your strengths.

6. Do what you do best – and do it the best that you can.

7. Remember who pays your wages.

CASE STUDIES

Stan discovers the real world of the self-employed

Stan was made redundant because the company he worked for went bust. He is a maintenance engineer for boilers and central heating systems. He had enough contacts to build up his own customer list, so he decided to work for himself.

He has a good rapport with his customers and potential customers, and he quickly builds up a base of regular customers. He also builds up a good relationship with suppliers. What he finds difficult, however, is the administration and bookkeeping. His wife steps in to help him out, by doing the typing of correspondence and the bookkeeping in the evenings. After a couple of years, Stan has built up so many customers that he can take on an employee to work for him, and his wife can afford to give up her part-time job to work for him, doing his administrative jobs and bookkeeping.

POINTS TO CONSIDER

1. Imagine you have built up a good rapport with a customer who gives you a lot of work. You struggle to keep up to date with your bookkeeping, however. You are now one day away from the deadline to send in

your VAT return. If it is late, you may face paying a fine. You have set aside the day and evening if necessary to finish off your VAT return. But then the customer rings up, asking you to do a rush job, which is extremely urgent, and without which he will be in trouble. He is willing to pay you a higher rate for the job. Do you put the customer first, and incur a fine for the late VAT return?

2. What are your strengths?

3. Are you able to get any help in doing the jobs you don't like or are not good at?

(3)

Starting Out

So, you have taken the plunge, and decided to start working for yourself. Congratulations! You will probably find that you have now started to work for the hardest boss you have ever had! Where do you go from here?

The first thing to realise is that you are actually running a business. Many people do not think of self-employment as running a business. Make that connection, and you will have a running start.

In any business, knowledge is power. So what do you need to know? I would suggest three things:

1. Know your product or service.
2. Know your customers.
3. Know your competitors.

KNOWING YOUR PRODUCT OR SERVICE

We have already seen that the customer is king. The customer pays your wages – that cannot be repeated too many times. But you must have something to sell the customer. It may be a product, goods or a service. Whatever it is, make sure that you know everything there is to know about it.

Certain goods (or ranges of goods) or services may be so varied that it is impossible to know everything about them. If so, try to specialise, and find out as much as you can about your speciality.

There are several ways to do this. Whatever your trade or profession there is bound to be a professional body or trade organisation for it. Join up. That association will be able to give you support in all sorts of ways. One of the most important is in providing means of further study or training.

Further training will become a way of life when you are self-employed. Knowledge, laws and technology are changing fast in every walk of life. It is vital to keep up to date. You will find that the more you learn about your subject, the more it will help you. Just one aspect may suggest a way in which you can expand the range of products or services you supply to your customers.

What are you supplying?

One area that applies more specifically to services rather than products is the way in which you think of the service you are providing. The way in which you think of it will also be the way in which the customer perceives it. Often our thinking is too conventional. We think about our services in terms of the activity we do.

Stop now, and think about the activity you carry out. How would you describe it? Do you supply cleaning services, or bookkeeping services, or public relations services? Whatever it is, the answer was probably in those terms – based on the activity.

> **Why not think about your service as providing solutions to your customers' problems?**

It may take a little practice to think about your activity in a new way, and it applies differently for different kinds of activities. But a new way of thinking can lead to a new way of approaching how you supply your services to customers, and how you approach the business of attracting new customers.

KNOWING YOUR CUSTOMERS

It is important to know your product or service. It is just as important to know your customers. After all, you cannot churn out something in a vacuum, if there is nobody to sell to. So make it your business to know as much as you can about your customers.

Find out all you can about your existing customers. If, for example, you are running a shop, find out how many times per week or month your customers come in. Find out what their shopping pattern is – what times of day they come in, how visits to your shop fit in with visits to other shops. Find out all you can about their shopping habits, for your type of goods, and for other types of goods. Find out what makes them come to you for the goods you sell.

Perhaps you do not sell to the general public. Yours may be a product or service that you sell to other businesses. Find out about those businesses – why they buy from you, what kind of things they sell, how they operate. You will not be able to become as much of an expert about their business as you are about your own. However, the more you know about their business, the easier it is to sell to them.

Find out all you can about potential customers. If you want to increase your business, try to target a certain type of customer. Then find out all you can about that type of person or company. Especially, try to find out why they do not buy from you now.

KNOWING YOUR COMPETITORS

Another important area to find out about is the competition. There are very few who have a monopoly of the trade in their product or service in their geographical area. And you can be sure that if a monopoly exists, somebody will soon come along, offering the same or a similar thing, and try to improve on what is presently on offer.

You do not have to be at loggerheads with your competitors. Most people have a good relationship with their trade competitors, and recognise that competition is a simple economic fact of life. In fact, competition is a good thing for trade and business generally.

In any city, town or geographical area, there will probably be enough room for several people providing the same product or service. They can happily co-exist side by side. As we have seen in recent years with airlines, if one big player tries to eliminate the competition, it is not long before another competitor comes in with a new idea, or a new presentation. In most towns or areas, there are associations of people in the same business. They recognise that there is room for them all, and that there are many things they can do together for their common good. For example, in seaside towns or tourist areas, local hoteliers' associations or tourist boards flourish.

Finding out all you can about your competitors helps you to know about the way your business is carried on in your area, about the general pricing structure, business terms, and so on. Of course, your competitors are not going to give you all their most sensitive information about their customers, products, etc., but it should be possible to get enough information to have a pretty good idea of what is going on.

CHECKLIST

1. Know all you can about your specialist area.

2. Think creatively about the way you present your product or service.

3. Know your customers inside out.

4. Find out all you can about potential customers.

5. Join local associations.

6. Find out all you can about your competitors.

CASE STUDIES

George and Mildred take on a pub

George and Mildred have always wanted to own their own pub. George has worked as a barman, so he has a good start in knowing something about the licensed trade. Mildred enrols on a commerical catering course, to learn about catering, since that will make up a substantial part of the pub trade. They start frequenting the pub they want to run, to find out all they can about the regulars. They also visit other pubs in the same town, and round about, to get other ideas on the sort of things that work in other places.

Fred conducts a survey

Fred carries out industrial cleaning contracts. He is just reaching the point where he could buy a new van and take on somebody to work for him, but to justify it financially he needs more customers. He starts by finding out all about the cleaning needs of his existing customers. He then designs a survey and sends it to all the other factories, warehouses, etc. on the various industrial estates in his town.

As he expected, the response rate to his survey was not good, but he follows up the replies he gets. From this follow up, he gets enough new customers to justify the new van and taking on a new person.

POINTS TO CONSIDER

1. Do you think you know enough about your job?

2. Does your job have areas you could specialise in?

3. How could you find out more about your existing customers?

4. How could you find out more about potential new customers?

5. How could you find out more about your competitors?

Succeeding and Growing

If you can meet with triumph and disaster,
and treat those two impostors just the same...

Rudyard Kipling

PLANNING AND BUDGETING

If we substitute 'success and failure' for 'triumph and disaster', we can see that Rudyard Kipling's sentiments are not in tune with modern feelings. Everyone wants to succeed. But how do you know whether you have succeeded or not? What are the measures of success?

The key aim of being in business on your own account is to make a living. In financial terms this means making a profit. Profitability is the one measure above all of success, and it is the key to survival.

The key is to make plans, put figures on your plans, then monitor your results against your plans. Only then can you take any effective action to correct what is going wrong, or take any other action to achieve your targets.

Working without plans or budgets is like shooting an arrow at a wall without a target painted on it. You are virtually certain to hit the wall. If the mood took you, you could then paint a target round the arrow and say you had hit the target.

Planning and budgeting are particularly important at two stages of a business:

1. starting up
2. growing.

Starting up

When you start up, you may be uncertain about many things, such as:

- How much will I need to sell to break even?
- Can I do it all on my own?
- If not, what help do I need?
- Will I need to borrow any money – if so, how much?

In order to answer these questions, you must make plans, and formalise these plans into budgets.

Growing

When you start expanding, it may involve taking on employees (or more employees), moving to bigger premises, or borrowing more money. The key factor in expansion is nearly always management of working capital. This is one of the most important elements of running a business.

'Managing working capital' may sound very grand, but its result is very simple to understand and to appreciate – cash flow.

> **More businesses fail because of cash flow problems than because of poor profitability.**

So let's take a look at working capital and why it is so important.

MANAGING WORKING CAPITAL

Any business has assets and liabilities. A balance sheet of a business shows its assets and its liabilities. The excess of assets over liabilities represents the total capital of the business. If there is an excess of liabilities over assets, there is a capital deficit, and the business is said to be insolvent. But the total capital of the business is not the same as the working capital.

To discover the working capital of a business, the assets and liabilities are broken down into current and long-term items. The normal way these are shown is:

Assets –   fixed assets
             current assets
Liabilities – long-term liabilities
             current liabilities

Fixed assets

As the name implies, these are assets that are fixed, i.e. they are held for the long term. They include equipment, vehicles, land and buildings, etc.

Current assets

These are assets that change from day to day in the course of business. They include the bank balance, money owed from customers, stock of goods or materials, expenses paid in advance, etc.

Long-term liabilities

These are items that are not payable until some time into the future – the usual measure of this is items payable after one year in advance. They include long-term loans, etc.

Current liabilities

These are items that are payable currently – the usual measure is up to one year ahead. These would include the normal trade accounts, the current instalments on repayments of things like hire purchase debts, etc.

Measuring working capital

The measure of working capital is the difference between current assets and current liabilities.

Let's look at an example. Figure 1 shows a summary of a business's assets and liabilities. In this form, all it shows is the total net assets.

Balance sheet – John and Mary's Dairy		
Assets		
Vehicles	6,000	
Equipment	5,000	
Premises	50,000	
Stock	10,000	
Debtors	3,000	
Expenses paid in advance	2,000	
Bank balance	5,000	
		81,000
Liabilities		
Creditors	6,000	
Accruals	1,000	
H.P. account	3,000	
Mortgage	30,000	
		40,000
Total net assets		£41,000

Fig. 1. John and Mary's Dairy's balance sheet (1).

However, Figure 2 shows the same information in a different form, and we can now see the working capital (D) as well as the total net assets.

So why is the working capital so important? To answer this, try to think of it in a different way. If you buy stock, or pay your insurance for a year in advance, you are 'tying up' your money. You have spent that money and you cannot get it back. Or can you? You can turn that money into sales to your customers, and get it back, with the value you have added to it, i.e. your profit. However, before you get that money back, time has elapsed. You have had to buy your stock, then process it into the finished product to sell to your customers, then actually make the sale, and finally wait to be paid.

Balance sheet – John and Mary's Dairy			
Assets:			
Fixed assets			
Vehicles	6,000		
Equipment	5,000		
Premises	50,000		
		61,000	A
Current assets			
Stock	10,000		
Debtors	3,000		
Expenses paid in advance	2,000		
Bank balance	5,000		
	20,000		B
Current liabilities			
Creditors	6,000		
Accruals	1,000		
H.P. account	3,000		
		10,000	C
Working capital		10,000	D
		71,000	
Long-term liabilities			
Mortgage		30,000	E
Total net assets		£41,000	F

Fig. 2. John and Mary's Dairy's balance sheet (2).

Question and answer
Surely this problem about working capital would not affect
retail businesses? After all, retail businesses sell direct to
the public, and they do not give credit to their customers.

It might seem at first sight that this problem does not exist
if you are a retailer. After all, you buy in bulk, then sell
the items individually, and the customer pays at the time
he buys the goods. But of course, you have to stock the
shelves of your shop to attract the customers, and you
cannot sell all your goods at once. So the money 'tied up'
is the stock that is sitting on your shelves. At any one time,
you will probably have several thousand pounds' worth of
goods in your shop. If you ever let this diminish, people
stop coming in your shop.

So, you have money tied up in:

- stock – either for resale or as raw materials to be
  processed
- work in progress, i.e. in an intermediate state not yet
  ready to be sold
- debts owing to you from customers
- expenses paid in advance.

However, as well as having money owed to you by
customers, you may also owe money to suppliers or other
creditors. To a certain extent, this offsets the money you
have tied up. But there will always be a balance
remaining, and this is your working capital. Because this
money is tied up, you have to finance it somehow.

Maintaining the working capital

So far, we have looked at the working capital as a 'snapshot' at a particular moment. But your business does not stand still, and as we saw earlier, the current assets and current liabilities change from one day to the next in the course of your business.

Therefore, you have to reckon with the fact that the working capital is a continuous requirement. At any time, you will have money owing to your creditors, and you will have a certain level of stock, of work in progress, and of debts owing to you from your customers.

If:

 ◆ your business continued at an absolutely steady rate
 ◆ your sales were exactly the same every month
 ◆ your customers took exactly the same time to pay you every month, and
 ◆ you kept exactly the same level of stock at all times

then you could be sure that your working capital requirement would stay the same.

But life isn't like that. Your working capital requirement is likely to fluctuate due to the thousand and one little changes to the course of your business.

The most obvious reasons for changes in your working capital requirement are:

 ◆ seasonal variations

- unexpected one-off occurrences
- an expanding business.

Seasonal variations

Certain trades, or businesses in certain locations (such as holiday areas), experience seasonal variations. So if, for example, a clothing manufacturer has sales which, year after year, are 'clustered' at two or three different months of the year, he cannot simply engage staff for those times, then let his factory and machinery stay idle for the rest of the year. Instead, he tries to even out his production throughout the year, stockpile the goods, then sell them all at the regular selling seasons.

What this means is that for most of the year, he has to pay wages, buy in the raw materials, and keep his factory running. He gets paid much later. In the meantime he has to finance everything.

Unexpected one-off occurrences

Sometimes, if you are doing your job particularly well, you may get an enquiry from an unexpected source. 'Can you take on this job?' The job may seem like the chance of a lifetime. It could be very profitable, and may have the potential of leading to other things.

In itself, it is a good thing, and it may be too good to turn down. But you have to count the cost. They want the job done immediately.

- Are you able to postpone other jobs for regular, established customers?

- Will you need to buy in extra stock or equipment?
- Will you have to employ extra people?
- What are the payment terms?
- Will you have to wait longer for your money?

So, although taking it may be the right thing, you might have to finance an extra working capital requirement temporarily.

An expanding business

If your business is expanding, it is easy to do the mathematics and see that the gap between the money owing by you and the money tied up will also increase. Failure to take this into account is the reason for the collapse of many businesses when they are in this expansion phase.

When your business is expanding, you must make even more detailed plans and budgets. An uncontrolled expansion is one that is likely to fail. Expansion plans tend to show that expansion does not happen smoothly, like a smooth upward line on a graph. Instead, the graph tends to show 'steps' when there is a sudden need for extra resources of some sort. For example, you may be able to expand to a certain point in your present premises. But after that point is reached, you will need new premises. Now, premises are not a resource you can 'turn on' like a tap. You have to plan ahead to buy or rent new, bigger premises. The actual changeover will inevitably involve a break in the normal production, and there will be a hiatus when reorganisation takes place.

All this will mean a greatly increased working capital requirement.

Appreciating the importance of working capital

By now, you should realise the importance of working capital. But here is the heart of the matter – **for the vast majority of businesses, you cannot finance your own working capital**. You will have to borrow in some form or another. The usual way of financing working capital is by a bank overdraft. This is the most flexible form of finance for this purpose. As your customers pay you, and you pay your suppliers and employees, your bank balance fluctuates from day to day. An overdraft means that you only pay interest on the credit you actually use. Interest is calculated on the day-to-day balance. You must, of course, be careful to keep within your agreed overdraft limit. Banks tend to charge exorbitant rates of interest on unauthorised overdrafts.

As we shall see in a later chapter, your bank will want to know your plans before giving you an overdraft facility. This will include seeing your written plans, including budgets and cash flow forecasts, and then regular monitoring of your actual performance against budgets and forecasts.

Making your plans and budgets

Setting out your plans
The first thing to do is to write out in a narrative form what you hope to achieve, and try to be as precise as possible. Put into this plan the numbers and dates. Try to see as far ahead as you can. Then work out how you will

achieve it. Again, be as precise as possible. Break down your plan into as many parts as you can, both in terms of the timing and of the resources to be used.

Making budgets
Next, turn those plans into a formalised budget. You may need help from your accountant to do this. This will set out the plans in terms of a profit and loss account. There may be other stages before this is reached, but that is the end product. Alongside this, there will probably be a 'Capital Budget' showing the planned expenditure on assets such as equipment, vehicles, buildings, etc., and the timing of that expenditure.

Forecasting your cash flow
The next stage will be a cash flow forecast. We have already seen how important is the management of working capital. The practical outworking of that is in cash flow. The cash flow forecast takes the figures from the plans and budgets, then breaks them down by the expected timing of the inflow and the outflow of cash. Figure 3 shows an example of a cash flow forecast. These are usually calculated with monthly rests, and show the forecast bank balance or overdraft at the end of each month. In Figure 3, the bank overdraft is forecast to go from £1,500 at the beginning of the year to £1,600 at the end. However, on the way, it is forecast to peak to £8,000 in August.

You have probably already realised that the next step is to compare the actual performance against these budgets and forecasts. It is relatively easy to compare the actual bank overdraft at the end of each month with the forecast

	Jan	Feb	Mar	Apr	May	Jun	Jul	Aug	Sep	Oct	Nov	Dec
Cash inflow												
Sales – credit customers	2000	1500	2000	2500	3000	3500	2500	2000	3000	5500	6500	5000
cash	1800	1700	1900	1800	2000	2500	2200	2500	2800	3000	2600	1600
Other income			500			600			500			400
Private loan								2000				
Loan from bank								4000				
	3800	3200	4400	4300	5000	6600	4700	10500	6300	8500	9100	7000
Cash outflow												
Goods for resale	2200	2200	3000	2600	2500	3200	3400	3000	3000	3000	2900	2800
Wages for staff	400	500	500	500	500	500	500	500	1000	1000	1000	1000
Overheads	400	500	800	500	600	800	600	800	900	1200	1100	1000
Own drawings from business	1000	1000	1000	1000	1000	1000	1000	1000	1000	1200	1200	1200
Tax payments	1000						1000					
Purchase of van and equipment								8000				
Net cash inflow	5000	4200	5300	4600	4600	5500	6500	13300	5900	6400	6200	6000
Net cash outflow	1200	1000	900	300	400	1100	1800	2800	400	2100	2900	1000
Opening overdraft	1500	2700	3700	4600	4900	4500	3400	5200	8000	7600	5500	2600
Closing overdraft	2700	3700	4600	4900	4500	3400	5200	8000	7600	5500	2600	1600

Fig 3. John and Mary's Dairy's cash flow corecast.

figure. That is why the banks are so keen on seeing your cash flow forecast.

MONITORING RESULTS

> **If you can't measure it, you can't control it.**

Once you have made your plans and budgets, they are useless if they just sit in a drawer unopened. In fact, they are worse than useless, because they have cost you a lot of time and effort, and possibly professional fees. You must monitor your results, i.e. compare your actual achievements with your plans. Any variation, either way, should be investigated.

But even that is not enough. Again, seeing the results and even knowing the reason for the variation is worse than useless if it does not result in any action. The information must be acted upon.

Accounting for results

It is obvious that in order to monitor the results, you must have an adequate accounting system. It does not have to be over-elaborate – rather it should be appropriate to the business you are carrying out. In these days of computerisation, any business however small should be able to account for its transactions regularly. However, there are still many businesses which successfully account for their business by a manual system.

> **If it does the job, and it ain't broke, don't fix it.**

It should also be able to deliver figures that correspond with the way in which the budget has been prepared. This makes the comparison process easy. The key to the usefulness of accounts is their regularity and promptness. An unsophisticated manual system can be far more effective than a sophisticated computerised system, if it is regularly and promptly kept, while the computerised system is only written up once in a blue moon.

It is better to have figures produced on the day that at 90% correct than figures that are 100% correct, but produced four weeks late.

Taking action

As we have seen, it is useless to produce figures then make no use of them. But before you act on the figures, make sure you know what they mean. It is easy to think the figures are pointing in one direction, when they are not. So think about asking advice, perhaps from your accountant, if:

- you are uncertain about the figures
- they seem to show a large difference from expectations
- they seem to indicate drastic action is needed.

You must be able to work out what action is needed from the figures. If your figures are structured properly, you should be able to pinpoint where things are going wrong, or what action is needed. Here are some ways in which the figures may show what action is needed:

- You are losing sales because you do not have the right stock. This could be due to several factors. Are you simply misjudging what your customers want? Are you unable to get supplies because you have not paid your suppliers promptly enough?

- There is a build up of work in progress on the factory floor. Are some jobs getting left in a half finished state? Is something delaying their progress (e.g. machinery breakdown)?

- Customers are not paying in the expected time. Is your credit control adequate?

- Are you taking too much out of the business?

MARKETING

If you are to grow, you must do it by a controlled process. Growth which just 'happens', like Topsy, can be worse than useless. It can be positively harmful. To grow in a controlled way, you must concentrate on marketing and selling your product or service. So what exactly is marketing? Here are some of the ways in which it is perceived:

- advertising
- pricing
- promotions
- finding the right customer base
- dealing with complaints
- thinking up new ways of selling
- projecting the right image.

Marketing is none of these in isolation, although it can

include all of these activities, and more. The one definition of marketing which sums it all up is:

> **Marketing is any activity which
> makes selling easier, or even unnecessary.**

Question and answer
How can selling be rendered unnecessary?

By seeing the vital difference between buying and selling. The ultimate 'heaven' for a business is that you do not have to sell at all – people come to you wanting to buy your product or service.

Consider this famous quotation:

> If a man write a better book, preach a better sermon or make a better mousetrap than his neighbour, though he build his house in the woods, the world will make a beaten path to his door.
> (Attributed to Ralph Waldo Emerson)

In order to get 'the world to make a beaten path' to your door, the world must know about your mousetrap, and why it is better than your neighbour's. This is the job of marketing.

Some marketing activities are 'overt', while others are 'covert'. Let's look at some of the more 'covert' activities first.

Projecting the right image
This is perhaps one of the first things to do in marketing,

and it may well be something you do almost subconsciously. However, it is an area about which you must think and make positive decisions. The image you project of your product, or your service, is ultimately about your personal image. You must make a conscious decision about the image you want to project, because that image impacts directly on the sort of customers you will reach.

For example, *The Sun* and *The Times* are two very different newspapers, projecting different images. They attract different kinds of readers. What you must decide is which type of market you are aiming at.

Do not be tempted to make value judgements about your target market. In commercial terms, there is no 'better' type of customer. Many services and products are aimed at the *Sun* reader rather than the *Times* reader. As long as the marketing and the product or service coincide, then the result is good business.

So, decide on your image, and do everything you can to build up that image – starting with your personal image.

Remember that many elements contribute to an image. Think about the name you will give your business. Is it to be something traditional – like 'Mary Smith, hairdresser', or something like 'Making Waves'? You will probably need to get some letterheads printed, so what about a logo? If you cannot design one yourself, get a graphic designer to help. What about a website? It is likely that your town or city has a website, and you can benefit by getting yourself on that website. You can also have your own independent website.

However, try not to make it too sophisticated or complicated.

Pricing

Many people do not realise that the pricing of their products or services is a marketing decision. To you, the provider, the factors that you think of in deciding pricing are the ones that concern your ability to provide the product or service – your costs, in other words. But try thinking from the buyer's point of view.

- Some people buy regardless of the price.
- Some people buy on impulse.
- Some people buy because the product is perceived as cheap – others because it is perceived as expensive.
- Some people buy without even knowing the price.

Finding the right customer base

Marketing research means finding out as much as you can about your potential customers. There may be many ways of doing this. There are, for instance, businesses which specialise in providing lists of potential customers sorted by whatever criteria you determine. However, you do not need expensive solutions to this problem. You can simply find out what you need to know by asking.

A local trade directory, perhaps *Thompson's* or *Yellow Pages*, will yield a good starting point for finding the addresses and phone numbers of businesses which could be your targets.

Dealing with complaints

Do not try to kid yourself that you will never get

complaints. However good your product or service is, something is invariably going to go wrong at some time – we are all human, and we all make mistakes.

When handling mistakes, remember again – the customer is king. Never make the customer feel at fault or to blame. Even if you feel that the complaint is unjustified, give the customer your time and patience. Don't lose your cool. Even if you feel the customer is wrong, make some offer to put right what they perceive is wrong. This could be by replacing the item, or giving the customer a credit for future purchases, or even in extreme cases, giving them more than they feel they have lost.

It is better to be wrong yourself, and retain the customer, than to be right and lose the customer.

> **Customers who have had a complaint satisfactorily resolved are more loyal than those who have never had a complaint.**

Advertising, public relations and promotions

These are all 'overt' methods of marketing which are valid in themselves, but do not have to make up the whole of your marketing effort. One thing all 'overt' marketing activities have in common is that they can cost a lot of money.

When you are starting up or expanding, give yourself a budget for advertising and promotion and stick to it. Do not think you necessarily have to spend a lot of money on consultants or advertising.

For instance, you can do much of the public relations work yourself. Find out what trade journals and local journals and newspapers there are, and send them any press releases you can write. Local papers, in particular, are very receptive to news items about local businesses.

If you are going to display at exhibitions or carry out special promotions, plan these carefully. You do not necessarily need to have expensive display material, but whatever you have must be well presented and present you in as high a profile as possible.

SELLING

As we have seen, you must learn the vital difference between your selling something to customers, and their buying from you. As we have also seen, you must do everything with the attitude of 'the customer is king'. Your life blood is sales. More than that, you cannot just sit back on an established customer base and expect it to provide all your needs.

Nothing ever stands still. The only thing that is guaranteed is change. Old customers die, or move away. They must be replaced with new customers. After you have been selling in a certain market place for a while, you find that the 'pool' from which your customers come is different, whether that 'pool' is a geographical location, or some other identifiable group of customers. Conditions change, people's expectations change, people's tastes change. We will look at responding to change later in this chapter. The important point is that you must constantly be seeking:

1. new customers, and
2. new ways of selling to existing customers.

It may sound 'old hat', but if you are not going forward, you are going backward, just like trying to go up the down escalator. You must be geared to selling – it is the force which drives your business. Nowhere is this more true than when you are expanding.

INNOVATING

Almost as important as the sales drive is the need to keep innovating. If you try to retain your customer base with the same product or service, that customer base will gradually dry up.

You must make sure you are technically up to date with all the latest trends, technology, marketing ideas, etc. that affect your industry or profession. Spend time regularly reading relevant trade magazines, visiting trade exhibitions, and simply thinking about your product or service.

There is no reason at all why you should simply 'catch on' to ideas generated by somebody else. If you are thinking all the time about what your customers want, or trying to anticipate what they will want in the future, then you may well come up with some new ideas. If you do get an idea, try to nurture it. Write it down, discuss it with colleagues, think about possible drawbacks. In short, develop the idea.

Only when you have exhausted all the thinking, try it out. It may fail, yes. But it is better to have tried and failed than never to have tried. Even if the idea as a whole fails, it usually has the germ of an idea which is valid, and can be used in some other context.

RESPONDING TO CHANGE

One characteristic of all successful businesses is that they are driven by enthusiastic champions of change. At the risk of repeating this point, conditions are changing around us all the time, and if you do not respond to change, your business will gradually wither and die. You cannot stand still. Many professionals are confidently predicting that in five years time, 60% of the income of your business will come from products or services that you do not currently provide.

To take this concept even further, you must be proactive rather than reactive. Do not just respond to changes by keeping up to date with them. Why not be the instigator of changes? This can apply to many areas of your business, including:

- new products
- new services
- new technologies of production
- new technologies of communication
- new ways of selling to your customers
- new ways in which your customers can pay you
- new working patterns for you and your staff.

ADMINISTRATION

The emphasis in this chapter so far has been on the creative side of your business – think up new ideas, new ways of doing things, go out and get new customers, develop new products and services, and so on.

However, there has to be a disciplined side to your business life. Your administration must be adequate. This means record keeping, which includes:

- bookkeeping
- stock control
- employee and PAYE records
- VAT records
- customer files
- supplier files
- income tax records
- product development and records.

Administration and bookkeeping are looked at in more detail in Chapter 11. Suffice it to say here that without adequate administration you will neither succeed nor grow.

CHECKLIST

1. Make your plans, turn them into figures, then monitor the results.
2. Actively manage working capital.
3. Market yourself.
4. Know the difference between buying and selling.
5. Keep on innovating.
6. Keep alert to change.
7. Don't let the administration slip.

CASE STUDIES

John and Mary's Dairy grows

John and Mary are a husband and wife in partnership, trading as a dairy. They have the chance to take on a new contract to supply school canteens in their town. They are tempted to say 'yes' straight away without thinking about it. After all, it seems to be the opportunity they have been waiting for, after all the years of hard work.

They talk to their accountant, who shows them that they must consider several vital issues:

- Can they continue to work from their existing premises?
- Will they need any new or extra machinery or vehicles?
- Will they have to take on any more staff?
- What are the payment terms for the school contract?
- Will they need to ask the bank for an increased overdraft limit?
- Will they need to finance the purchase of new equipment or vehicles by loan, or hire purchase, or leasing?

They prepare, with their accountant's help, a business plan for their business, anticipating the extra business generated by the new contract. The plan includes:

- a narrative of the new opportunity
- a summary of the main terms of the proposed new contract
- a summary of the new capital expenditure needed

- a note of the extra staff needed
- a profit projection
- a cash flow forecast
- a proposal for borrowing from the bank.

This plan is the basis for the meeting with their bank manager. The bank agree to the proposal, giving them a loan over five years to purchase extra machinery and a vehicle, and an increased overdraft limit to be reviewed annually. The conditions for the loan include preparation of regular management accounts, to be submitted to the bank at quarterly intervals.

POINTS TO CONSIDER

1. How would you know if you are succeeding or not? By the size of your bank balance? Or do you measure success by other criteria?

2. Do you want your business to grow? Do you agree that if you are not going forward, you are really going backward?

3. Have you calculated your 'worst case scenario'? Could you survive it, or would you need to go cap in hand to the bank?

4. What do you foresee as the three major changes in your trade or profession in the next three years?

5. What new product or service could you sell your customers?

5

Choosing the Format

Becoming self-employed can happen in several ways. There is a choice of formats. Each of these has its advantages and disadvantages.

LIMITED COMPANY

A limited company is a separate legal entity from its members. The business is actually owned by the limited company, not you. This has its advantages and its drawbacks. As the name suggests, the liability of the company is limited. If there were a failure, therefore, you and your personal assets would be protected. This is in contrast to the position where you are a sole trader or in partnership. In those cases, you have unlimited liability.

Who owns the company?

The ownership of a commercial company is determined by the ownership of the shares in the company. It is possible to have just one shareholder, but this is not recommended. Shareholdings in a company are a good way to pass on ownership of the business gradually, say, to the next generation of your family. There can be different classes of shares, giving different rights. So you could, for example, give non-voting shares to someone who wishes to put some money into the company, but who does not wish to have any part of the management of the business.

The ownership of a company is separate from the management of the company. A company must have at least one director and one secretary. Again, it is recommended that there are at least two directors. However, the directors do not have to be shareholders of the company.

Becoming a director

If you run your business in the format of a limited company, technically you become employed again. You receive a salary as director, and this makes your category employed rather than self-employed. However, this is a technicality, which respects the legal fiction of a company being a separate legal entity from its owners. In all other respects, you are working for yourself. What this means, however, is that you have to pay tax under PAYE, and you have to pay class 1 National Insurance. Some of the class 1 National Insurance is deducted from your salary, and some is borne by the company as the employer's share. Having said this, the class 1 contributions do entitle you to an earnings related supplement to your retirement pension.

You can also pay yourself dividends on the shares which you hold. The dividends must be paid to all holders of the same class of shares. Dividends are subject to a tax credit of 10%, and if you do not pay higher rates of tax, there is no further tax to pay on dividends. However, you may not reclaim the tax credit as a repayment to you.

Company taxation

The company pays corporation tax on any profits (after

paying you the director's salary). The rate of corporation tax goes from 0% to 32.75%, depending on the amount of profit made. This is lower than the personal rates of income tax. It may, therefore, be advantageous to pay corporation tax if the level of profit is right, and if you need to keep the profits inside the company (for example, for reinvestment in assets). If you want to take the money out of the company, the best method is usually a mixture of director's salary and dividends.

Company law

A company is governed by company law, mainly as contained in **The Companies Act 1985**. There are strict time limits (with penalties for failure) for filing documents, including the company accounts, at Companies House, and members of the public can search the records and the accounts of any company. Directors are subject to regulations, and can be fined or even found guilty of a criminal offence for failure to comply.

PARTNERSHIP

A partnership is legally defined as the connection between two or more people carrying on business together with a view to making profit. If you are going to carry on business with someone else, it is advisable to have the terms of the agreement agreed in the form of a written, signed partnership agreement. If there is no partnership agreement, the partnership is governed by the terms of **The Partnership Act 1890**.

A partnership often exists between husband and wife, where they share the business between themselves. In these cases, there is often no partnership agreement. If you are in partnership with another person or persons, you must make sure that you can work well with them, and that you each understand the basis on which you work.

This form can also be useful where you want to pass on the business to the next generation of your family. It is often useful in the case of husband and wife partnerships for tax planning purposes, i.e. to share the profit in such a way that the total tax bill of the couple is minimised. Each member of the partnership is liable to income tax and class 4 National Insurance on their share of the profit.

SOLE TRADING

This is the simplest form of carrying on your business. You can carry on a business on your own account.

You decide your own future, and have nobody to answer to. You are liable to income tax and class 4 National Insurance on your profits. You can employ anybody, including your wife or husband. The salary you pay to your spouse (or any member of your family) must actually be paid and evidenced, and it must be justified by the type of work, the responsibility and the number of hours worked.

MOVING BETWEEN DIFFERENT FORMATS

Having decided the format in which you carry on business, it is not set in stone for ever. You can change from one format to another with relative ease. It is not difficult for a sole trader to take on a partner, or to make his business into a limited company. A partnership may dissolve, and each partner continue to work on his or her own account. A partnership may also transfer its business to a limited company. Perhaps the most problematic is the liquidation of a limited company and the transfer of the business to an individual or a partnership.

FRANCHISING

This is a form of business in which you are the owner of the business, but the style and the name of the business is dictated by another person – or, more usually, company. A franchise involves operating a nationally or internationally known business under licence. The rewards can be good, and the support and training are usually good. It is in the interest of the franchisor as well as you, the franchisee, to make it a success, because the franchise payment to the franchisor is related to the sales or profit.

This form of business can be carried on in any format – sole trader, partnership, or limited company.

CHECKLIST

1. Weigh up the advantages and disadvantages of each format.

2. Choose the format which suits you best.

3. Be ready to change the format if your circumstances change.

CASE STUDIES

Christine starts a shop in partnership with her husband

Christine has the chance to start a small flower shop. Her

husband is also looking for a change, and is interested in horticulture. After much discussion, they set up in partnership, with Christine running the shop, while her husband does deliveries, looks at new products and business ideas, and does the administration.

They take advice from their accountant about the best way to share profits in order to save tax and National Insurance.

POINTS TO CONSIDER

1. How would you decide which format to choose?

2. How far ahead do you need to look to choose the right format?

3. Is passing on the business a particular issue for you?

Getting Help

Being your own boss can be a lonely thing. By nature, you may be an independent sort of person. But you will probably find that you appreciate any help you can get.

PROFESSIONAL HELP

Professionals charge for their services, and they are usually quite expensive. But for the right circumstances, they can more than earn their fees for you. The sort of professional help you might need as a self-employed person can include:

- **Solicitors** – for legal disputes, trade disputes, buying or selling property, employment problems, chasing slow paying debtors.

- **Estate agents** – for buying or renting premises, and reviews of rating assessments.

- **Architects** – for plans for extensions or new buildings.

- **Accountants** – for preparation of accounts, tax advice, compliance with regulations, tax returns, PAYE returns and VAT returns. Many accountants now see themselves as all-round business advisers, and market themselves as such. They can help with raising finance, 'health checks' on various aspects of the business, and providing regular management information to help you run the business better.

◆ **Business mentors** – The Business Volunteer Mentors Association is backed by the DTI, and provides the services of business people with experience to help in certain situations. The three most common areas where they can help are:

1. Pre-startup, to help people with an idea who want to turn it into reality.
2. Existing businesses looking to expand.
3. Businesses in trouble, needing a troubleshooter.

Make sure you get the right person. It should be firstly someone you trust and respect, and look also at his or her qualifications. Nobody can call himself or herself a solicitor unless they have the right qualifications and are registered with the Law Society. However, anybody can call himself or herself an accountant and set up an office in your high street. Chartered and Certified accountants have to undergo rigorous training, and they are subject to strict rules of ethical conduct and continuing education. This is not to say that an unqualified accountant cannot do a good job. But always find out as much as you can about any accountant or other professional. The best way to get referred to a professional is by personal recommendation from somebody you trust.

TRADE AND BUSINESS ASSOCIATIONS

Most towns have a chamber of trade or a chamber of commerce. These are associations that give mutual help and encouragement to each other. They are particularly helpful in fighting authorities or bigger companies where the well-being of the town as a whole is threatened. This can occur with things such as road widening schemes, parking restrictions, plans to charge for car parking, out of town developments, etc.

Your particular trade or profession will also doubtless have an association that represents you at a national or local level.

There are other bodies such as the Federation of Small Businesses, which campaigns on issues that affect small businesses. The British Franchise Association is a members' body for franchisees.

BUSINESS ANGELS

This type of help is given in conjunction with financial investment. It is the type of help where the person with money to invest also gives some time to offer technical or business experience, to help your business. This can be particularly helpful where your business is growing. Business angels are people with a lot of experience as well as some money to invest.

The National Business Angels Network can put you in touch with a business angel to suit you.

BUSINESS LINKS

There is a national network of Business Links. They are the private sector partnerships of Learning and Skills Councils, chambers of commerce, enterprise agencies and local authorities.

The Business Links can often provide subsidised consultancy, to help with such things as:

- raising money for growth
- exporting
- training
- managing change.

CHECKLIST

1. Get help from professionals for specific tasks or regular recurring work.

2. Join a local trade organisation for mutual support.

3. You might benefit from the help and involvement of a business angel.

4. Business links provide a wide range of subsidised help.

CASE STUDIES

April gets recommendations for her professional advisers

April is just starting as a self-employed person. She has located a shop where she can start her own antiques business. She has several connections in the antiques trade in her area. She asks them confidentially which solicitor and accountant they can recommend from their personal experience. One of the solicitors recommended is someone she had contact with over her father's will, so she decides to use that one.

She has never used an accountant before, and one name has been mentioned three times by contacts. She decides to get an initial interview, which the accountancy firm promote as a free interview if she signs up with them. She feels she can work with the accountant, and feels confident that he has much experience in dealing with antiques businesses.

POINTS TO CONSIDER

1. Do you feel that you can handle most things yourself? Or do you need help?

2. Do you think it is a good idea to get details of help available from professional sources and Business Links for reference?

3. Do you feel confident that you will know what help is available and when you will need it?

7

Anticipating Problems

Prevention is better than cure. In the life of any business there will be problems. If you can see what is coming, then they need not become crises.

SEEING YOURSELF THROUGH OTHER EYES

We can easily become blinded to our own shortcomings. Sometimes, other people can see a problem marching towards us that we miss. This may be due to getting so bogged down with the day-to-day running of the business. We keep our eyes down, looking at the everyday duties, but we sometimes need to look up, and see the bigger picture. That is where it is so useful to use someone else's eyes to see things about ourselves. So whose eyes can we use?

Getting help

There are several sources you can use to get other people's ideas and suggestions:

- professional advisers
- your bank manager
- trade or professional associations
- local groups
- courses and training sessions.

We saw the sort of help you can get in Chapter 6, so these do not need any expansion except to look at training. Just bear in mind that these people are there to help you, and they can often give you a different perspective on your business.

Courses and training sessions

Your local group or your trade or professional association will nearly always have details of courses and training. Do not neglect these. Laws and technology are constantly changing, and everybody working for themselves must keep up to date. Failure to do this is one of the prime causes of businesses failing. Further, failings of this sort happen gradually, as the rest of the world moves on, and you get left behind. So they are not easy to spot in the early stages.

Attending these courses and training sessions, you meet other people like yourself, trying to make a living as a self-employed person. Often these informal contacts are as useful as the formal part of the courses. Sometimes they can lead to long-term contacts, which are mutually beneficial.

READING THE DANGER SIGNS

Here are some of the danger signs to look out for – many of them are things which your accountant or bank manager would also look out for.

Avoiding an extravagant lifestyle

As Mr Micawber said, 'Annual income twenty pounds, annual expenditure nineteen, nineteen and six, result happiness. Annual income twenty pounds, annual expenditure, twenty pounds ought and six, result misery.' This simple guide to happiness is easy to apply when you are employed and receiving a regular wage packet. For the self-employed, however, it is not quite so simple. If you only prepare accounts once a year, you do not know what your annual income is. Your personal needs, however, have to be met month by month.

An obvious and easy guide is the state of your bank balance or overdraft. If you see a trend of an increasing overdraft month by month, that is a fairly clear sign that something is going wrong. Of course, you do have to take into consideration the underlying pattern – particularly if your business is seasonal. But it should be fairly clear what is happening.

Then, when your annual accounts are prepared, you will be able to see more precisely what profit you are making, and compare that to the money you are taking out to live on. In this context, if you are taking out more than your profit, you are being extravagant.

Always try to live within your means.

Don't put all your eggs in one basket
This simple rule applies to many areas of life. When you are working for yourself, it may not be easy to spot at first. But there are some ways it may affect you.

Too few customers
When you start out as self-employed, you may well have one customer only – it is not uncommon for this to be

your previous employer. However, try to expand your customer base as soon as you can. If you have a small number of customers, the failure of one of them will drastically affect your income. The more you have, the less would be the effect of one of them failing.

As you build up your customer base, you will also be able to be more discerning in the work you do. For instance, you may have the opportunity to accept offers of work from several customers. If you have a bigger choice, you can then choose the work which suits you best, or which is more remunerative.

Too few suppliers
If your business consists of selling goods or manufacturing goods of some sort, you need to buy in the goods to sell, or the raw materials to manufacture. Try to develop as many different sources of buying in as you can. This helps you in two ways:

1. You can have a bigger choice when ordering goods. You may be able to choose between different types or grades of materials, better delivery dates, and of course, you may have a better bargaining position to get the best deal available.

2. You are not so exposed to risk if one of your suppliers fails. If you only have one supplier, who fails, then your whole operation is in jeopardy. If you have other sources of supply, you do not come to a grinding halt.

Too few products or services
Try to diversify what you are selling as far as possible.

There is always bound to be a certain tension between diversifying and specialising. However, even if you are supplying a specialist product or service, to a niche market, you will probably be able to diversify to a limited extent.

The speed of technological change can only increase. Whatever your business, as we have seen, experts are predicting that:

In five years' time, over 60% of your income will come from goods or services that you do not presently supply.

This only serves to emphasise that you must keep up to date with all aspects of your trade or profession. Be ready for change. You may have one core element of your business, but the ways in which you carry that out, and the relative importance of it, are liable to change.

Insufficient backup

What if you encountered ill health, or sustained an accident? What backup do you have? If you are a one man band, there is little scope. However, many self-employed people have some kind of backup arrangement. They arrange with another person in the same business (i.e. a competitor) that if either person falls ill or has an accident, they will provide some level of cover for each other. As long as you can trust each other, this arrangement can be very helpful. It could mean the difference between your business surviving a period of ill fortune or not.

If your business is more than just a one man band, you may be able to get the backup you need from the people you already employ. You must also think about what would happen if a key member of staff fell ill or died. How would you cover the hiatus?

Insuring the risk

Think about insuring for these risks. You can get insurance to cover your income if you fall ill or have an accident. This may be needed to keep the business going in your absence, and to ensure that there is a business still there when you return to work. You can also get 'key person' insurance, to cover the absence or death of a key person in your business.

CHECKLIST

1. Try to see yourself as others see you.

2. Get help where you can.

3. Make full use of advisers.

4. Join business associations.

5. Keep up to date with training.

6. Don't live beyond your means.

7. Don't put all your eggs in one basket.

8. Get adequate backup.

CASE STUDIES

David takes advice

When David was called in to see his bank manager, he knew there was something wrong. He had been vaguely aware that his overdraft had gradually been increasing, year by year. However, he was still nowhere near hitting the limit of his overdraft, and did not look like doing so for a couple more years, so he did not worry.

The bank manager pointed out that his accounts showed he was making profits of about £16,000 for the last couple of years, but his withdrawals from the business were £20,000 last year, and £19,000 the year before that. His first reaction was to say that he was hardly being extravagant. He was still living on something just under the average national wage. However, after further discussion, he had to admit that he did not really keep any close check on his spending, and did not really know where the money was going.

The bank manager suggested he monitor his personal spending more closely. To that end, he installed a money program on his computer, and started to budget and monitor his spending. He now has it under control, and is able to live within his means.

POINTS TO CONSIDER

1. Do you think there is any possibility that your business may stagnate through not keeping up to date with the latest technology? If so, how would you go about keeping up to date?

2. Have you reviewed the 'worst case scenario' if anything should happen to you? Do you have adequate backup?

3. Do you make proper use of your accountant?

4. Are your efforts to get new customers enough? When did you last get a new customer?

8

Managing Your Resources

Unless he manages himself effectively, no amount of ability, skill, experience or knowledge will make an executive effective.

Peter Drucker

MANAGING YOURSELF

With one exception, people have different amounts of resources available to them when starting and developing their self-employment. This chapter will look at some of these. Firstly, however, the point must be made that you must learn to manage yourself. This involves many of the things touched upon in different parts of this book – such as building self-discipline, playing to your strengths, developing a positive attitude, and so on.

A common problem that many self-employed people encounter is that as their business develops and grows, they get so engrossed in it that the business starts to dictate their lives.

> **Take time out regularly to see where your life is going, and who is really in control.**

Here are four keys to managing yourself:

1. Firstly, that one word 'control'. Do not let other things or people dictate to you what you will do or how you will do it. If you find yourself in any difficulty, ask yourself first of all 'Who is in control here?' Once that angle is sorted out, other things fall into place much more easily.

As we have seen, this is fundamental:

> **If you cannot measure it, you cannot control it.**

Therefore, in learning to manage yourself, what is it you need to measure? The answer is, the achievement of your objectives. This involves three stages:

- ◆ Make your plans.
- ◆ Set goals and targets.
- ◆ Review the results.

When you have done these things, you can move on to the next stage:

- ◆ Make corrections and amend your plans.

This brings you back to the first step, and the whole process starts again. The process is continuous, and circular.

2. The next key to managing yourself is contained in this aphorism:

> **Learn to be effective – not efficient.**

It is relatively easy to become efficient at what you do. But do not fall into the trap of becoming extremely efficient at something which contributes little or nothing to your main goals. Learn to become effective – certain things may only take a moment's time, but they contribute more to your goals than other things which take much longer. Sort out the wheat from the chaff. In essence, this really means sorting out what are the important things, and concentrating on them. Some of these things need insight, and others come with experience.

3. Do not be afraid of making mistakes. The person who never made any mistakes never made anything.

4. *You* must make the decisions. Nobody else can make them for you. This is one of the big differences between working for somebody else and working for yourself – you have the final responsibility for making the decisions. It may come more easily to some people than to others. If you find it difficult, it is something that must be learnt – and take heart, it *does* get easier with experience. What you learn with experience is the kind of circumstance where a decision is needed. The worst thing of all is to avoid making a decision and letting things drift.

> **Remember – it is better to make a**
> **wrong decision than none at all.**

MANAGING YOUR TIME

Time is one thing which we all have the same amount of. It is also the most inelastic resource we have. The minute and hour hands move inexorably on, and cannot be manipulated. Think of time as a valuable resource, not to be wasted. This means actively managing your time, and if you have employees, managing their time.

The key to managing your time is planning. Do not just rush into each day, doing the next thing on your list. Whether you are a one man band, or an employer, set aside time to plan what is going to be done today, this week, this month, this year. Then take time out to check whether you have achieved all your targets.

What about interruptions?

It is all very well talking about an idealised world where you can plan ahead, and everything goes smoothly, but in the real world, things do not go smoothly. There are always interruptions which gobble up time. What to do about them?

1. Firstly, sort out the urgent interruptions from the non-urgent.

2. Next, sort out the important from the urgent. Just because something is urgent does not mean it is important.

3. If there is someone else, delegate the non-urgent and the non-important jobs.

4. Concentrate on the important jobs yourself. If there is nobody else, try to deal with the important things first, then the urgent things, then the non-urgent things.

GETTING EQUIPPED

Most jobs need some kind of equipment, and virtually every business will require transport of some kind to get you and your equipment round. Equipment can range from the smallest hand tools to the biggest computer-controlled machinery; transport can range from the oldest banger in the street to the biggest van or truck. The obvious advice is to get the best you can afford. But do not be tempted by the big, flashy hardware with all the knobs, bells and whistles you could ever want.

If a piece of equipment has lots of fancy features, ask yourself:

◆ How often would I use those extra features?
◆ Do they add to the possibility of breakdown?

Buy or hire?

If you need the equipment or vehicles permanently, there will not be any choice but to buy – although the method of financing it could involve a leasing contract. However, some items of equipment are not needed permanently, and can be hired as and when needed. Your local *Yellow Pages* have details of many equipment hire companies.

New or second-hand?

New equipment or vehicles obviously give you the best image and most would carry some sort of guarantee or warranty. The maintenance and repair costs would be likely to be much lower for the first few years. But not everybody – particularly those just starting out – can afford to buy new.

Many things can be very serviceable even when second-hand. A lot depends on the type of equipment. Ask yourself:

- Is it purely mechanical?
- Or is there a petrol or electrical motor?

Anything with a motor or engine is liable to break down. Find out as much as you can about:

- the use which the items have had
- how old they are
- the people who have used them
- why they are selling.

If you do not feel confident enough about judging the state of the equipment, try to find a friend who knows about it to help you.

Your local newspaper will often carry adverts for second-hand items, and the trade press often does also. The business pages of *Exchange and Mart* carry many items of business equipment, and you can also access them on the Internet at www.exchangeandmart.co.uk

FINDING PREMISES

Working from home
Not all businesses need special premises, and many self employed people start working from their own home. The obvious advantages are the convenience and the saving of expense. However, make sure of the following:

- **Insurance**. Your household insurance may well require you to notify them if you work from home. This is a change of material fact, and could affect the risk. If you do not do so, any claim you make could be rendered invalid.

- **Mortgage**. If you have a mortgage on your house, the mortgage company will hold the deeds. Make sure that there is no specific prohibition on working from home by the mortgage company.

- **Restrictive covenants**. Check the deeds of your house to make sure there are no restrictive covenants on the land, which would apply to working from home.

Working from your garden

If you cannot work in your home, you can always think about the possibility of a shed in the garden. This may sound inappropriate at first, but there are many suppliers which make 'garden offices', or 'garden workshops'. These can be of timber or block construction. Depending on the size of office or workshop you need, this could be a viable and economic alternative to renting office or workshop space.

Insurance and security are also factors to bring into account, however. Your garden office or workshop may not be as secure as your house, and you may have expensive equipment there. For that reason, the insurance companies will not normally include cover for this on your home insurance. You will have to take out an additional policy. But premiums can be anything up to 30% higher than they otherwise would be to take account of the less substantial nature of these structures.

Before you start this sort of project, check out the planning regulations. You may need special planning permission for this.

Finding premises – questions to ask

If you cannot carry on your self-employment from home, you will need to find appropriate premises. What is appropriate? It all depends on the type of business. Here are some questions to ask:

1. Do customers come to you, and spend time on your premises? Then make sure the premises are easily accessible, and as attractive as you can make them. Only you know the right degree of ambience and opulence to apply to your decor. You may put your customers off by creating the impression that they are paying extra for all the posh decor. You may put them off by having scruffy premises. Try to walk the thin line between.

2. Do you need to attract customers into the premises, or display goods in a shop window? If so, make sure you have adequate frontage.

3. Do you need to store goods on the premises? If so, make sure there is adequate space, and good access for unloading.

4. Are there any plans for the location? If so, do not commit yourself long term to a location that may be adversely affected by, say, an out of town shopping centre taking custom away, or a road change making it inaccessible.

5. Are there any competitors nearby?

6. Is there any assistance available from government or local authorities?

Planning permission

Make sure that the premises can be used for your purposes. Any commercial property should have a certificate for its approved uses. Certain changes of use within a class do not require planning permission. Planning permission is only usually refused if your operation would cause a nuisance, or a hazard to safety or health. However, mistakes can prove costly, so make sure of this aspect, and get help if you need it.

Building regulations

If the property needs any alterations, they will have to conform to the building regulations. Therefore, make sure the alterations comply.

Rent or buy?

Economic necessity will dictate whether you rent or buy your premises. In the long term, buying your premises often proves to be a good investment, but there is a lot of capital tied up in it. Renting premises can also create a long-term commitment, depending on the required term of the lease.

If you are renting, get a solicitor with commercial experience to look at the lease. Here are some of the issues to think about:

- How long is the term of the lease?
- What is the rent, and how often is the rent reviewed?
- What are the terms for reviewing the rent?

- Does the lease restrict the use of the property?
- Are there provisions that the landlord cannot unreasonably withhold consent for change of use?
- Can you sublet part of the premises?
- Can you sell your interest in the lease to someone else?
- Who is responsible for repairs and renewals?
- Who is responsible for decorating – interior and exterior?
- Is a premium payable 'up front'?
- Who pays for the cost of preparing the lease?

Finding out about the property

Whether buying or leasing, get advice from a reliable local surveyor or estate agent about the structural state of the property, its suitability for your business, and the valuation.

Find out also what the rates are on the property, and if there are any 'planning blights', i.e. future plans which might affect the viability of the premises.

Alternatives

As an alternative to finding premises of your own, serviced office space might be the answer. The concept is that serviced office space is the equivalent of a hotel, but instead of providing beds, they provide desks. The rents are usually more than straightforward offices, but they have some features which may just provide the right answer.

- There is usually no need to take out a long lease. They are let on licences, which means that they can provide for a much shorter period of notice.

◆ The 'service' element can provide many of the resources you would have to fund – often at a large initial outlay. For example, a typical serviced office would include a receptionist, office furniture, telephone lines, computers, etc.

A variation of this concept are 'telecottages'. These are based in rural areas, and they often include databases of local services available, including freelances, consultants, and suppliers of all sorts of goods and services. Training courses are also a feature of telecottages.

TAKING ON WORKERS

At some point, you may outgrow the 'one man band' stage of self-employment. There may also be an intermediate stage at which you cannot take on a permanent employee, but you may need to subcontract parts of your work, temporarily. Getting work done by an outside subcontractor is usually more expensive than employing someone. Yet there are many drawbacks to employing someone.

Becoming an employer

If you employ someone full time, or even part time, you take on many responsibilities. First of all, you have to pay a wage. That means making sure that you can pay your employee, month in, month out. There is a national minimum wage set by the government, with which you have to comply. In addition, there is an employer's National Insurance cost. The National Insurance for an employed person consists of two parts:

1. the employee's contribution, which you deduct from the employee's wages

2. the employer's contribution, which you as the employer have to bear.

If at any time you simply cannot pay your employee any longer, and you have to lay him or her off, you may incur a liability to redundancy pay. This is worked out on the basis of so many weeks' pay depending on the length of continuous service with you.

Complying with laws and regulations

If you want to employ anyone, you have to comply with many different laws and regulations. Here is a list of the most important:

♦ Employment Act 2002
♦ Trade Union and Labour Relations (Consolidation) Act 1992
♦ Race Relations Act 1976 and Race Relations (Amendments) Act 2000
♦ Equal Pay Act 1970
♦ Disability Discrimination Act 1995
♦ Rehabilitation of Offenders Act 1974
♦ Health and Safety at Work Act 1974.

Taking on obligations

You also take on various obligations, such as:

♦ The employee has the right to a written statement on the terms of employment.

- The employee is entitled to receive an itemised pay statement.
- You must take out compulsory employer's liability insurance.
- You are bound not to dismiss the employee unfairly.
- The employee cannot be prevented from joining a trade union.
- The employee must be given time off for certain functions, including public duties.
- You must operate a PAYE system to collect tax and National Insurance from the employee and pay it over to the government.
- You must also operate within your PAYE system the payment of:
  - statutory sick pay
  - statutory maternity pay
  - repayment of student loans
  - stakeholder pensions.

With all of these obligations, you might wonder if it is really worth taking on employees. If you subcontract your work out to a self-employed person, none of those obligations apply. Why not, then, simply decide that everyone who works for you is self-employed, and pay them as such, to avoid all the red tape? First of all, you cannot get someone to work for you substantially full time and simply call him or her self-employed. Understandably, the government, and in particular the Inland Revenue, are wise to this.

If you get someone to work for you, there is a distinction in law between a contract of service and a contract for services. On this distinction, the Inland Revenue bases its challenge to false claims to be self-employed. The following tests are applied to any claim to be self-employed:

- Do you work for one employer only, or several?
- Does your employer dictate your hours of work?
- Could you substitute somebody else to carry out the duties?
- Do you have to supply your own equipment?
- Do you carry any risk?
- Can you negotiate your rate of pay?

The consequences of a wrong course of action can be devastating. If you have been employing somebody, but treating them as self-employed, the Inland Revenue can challenge the practice. If they are successful, they can demand from you all the tax and National Insurance which you should have deducted. The Inland Revenue collect the money from you, and the onus is on you, as the employer, to recuperate it from the employee.

Learning the personal skills

Becoming an employer means that you have to manage the people working for you. You have to take some time out of doing the actual job yourself to oversee, control and motivate your workers. This comes naturally to some people. Many of the skills needed are intuitive, but many more can be learned. Even if you have a natural talent for getting on with people and managing them, you can still learn to do it better.

> **Learn how to create and lead a team.**

USING TECHNOLOGY

Advances in technology are accelerating all the time. The only thing we know about the future is that changes will come about ever more quickly. You would be ill advised to ignore these advances. However, do not be tempted to plunge into every latest new idea. Sometimes, existing technology is more appropriate to what you do.

For instance, despite the predictions that computer technology would make books obsolete, the book remains the most convenient format for reading fiction, poetry, education. Books are portable, easy to use, and they can be disposable or permanent.

On the other hand, many businesses now find that they are getting business advantages through being online. Others which ignore the Internet may well find themselves in gradual decline.

Lead or follow?

Some people take the attitude that they must be seen to be in the forefront of technological advance. They embrace all the latest advances. Others take the view that any new technology is usually overpriced at its inception, and rapidly combines increases in performance with reductions in cost. The experience of computers illustrates this attitude clearly. The time to embrace the new technology is after it has had time to get bedded in, and the problems sorted out.

Which stance you take depends on your personal attitude, your business, and the money you have available.

USING KNOWLEDGE AND IDEAS

We are living through the third great revolution – after the agricultural revolution and the industrial revolution has come the information revolution. The amount of information and knowledge available has exploded since the beginning of the twentieth century. The rate of increase keeps growing, and shows no sign of stopping.

Whatever your trade or business, knowledge is the key to success. As we saw in Chapter 3, knowledge is essential when starting out. But it does not stop there. For your business to continue, and to grow, you must keep on top of knowledge. Keep abreast of advances in your trade or business. Read about the latest news – in your trade, and in your locality. Make sure you are up to date with any laws or regulations relating to your trade or business.

As your business grows, your responsibility grows. You will need to sense when it is the right time to start delegating some of the responsibility in certain areas. You must make the judgement of when to buy in the skills you need. As your business grows, the over-riding skill you must learn is management of people.

Using the Internet

The Internet is a great source of information and ideas. You can also use it to grow and develop your business. There is a great opportunity to do much of your marketing and advertising online, and many smaller businesses are also set up to actually carry out their business online. The Index of Websites at the end of this book gives you a guided tour of many websites that may be useful to you.

> **The only thing that is certain is that nothing stands still. Changes will happen.**

Generating ideas

In the wake of knowledge come ideas. As you learn more, and keep abreast of developments, think about them. Do not just read passively, but think as you read. As you do so, you may well make connections between bits of knowledge from different sources. These connections can then become the germ of a new idea. It is on such ideas and connections that new business innovations and opportunities arise.

So never stop thinking – you could even generate a new product or service, and thus make a change yourself, which others will then read about.

DOING A SWOT ANALYSIS

This is a simple exercise. It involves making four lists, under the following headings:

1. Strengths
2. Weaknesses
3. Opportunities
4. Threats.

When you have identified as many items as you can under each heading, take action on them.

◆ **Build on your strengths**. Think how they can create new work or sales from existing customers, or attract new customers.

◆ **Eliminate your weaknesses**. Think about what measures you must take to eliminate weaknesses.

◆ **Take the opportunities**. If you can identify an opportunity, a competitor can do the same. If you do not take the opportunity, the competitor might do so.

◆ **Analyse the threats** to your profitability, and to your continued commercial existence. Take whatever corrective action is necessary.

CHECKLIST
1. Manage yourself.
2. Measure it and control it.
3. Be effective – not efficient.
4. Don't be afraid of making mistakes.
5. Take decisions.
6. Manage your time – it is your greatest resource.
7. Get equipped.
8. Find the right premises.
9. Know how to get people working for you.
10. Use technology appropriately.
11. Soak up knowledge and generate ideas.
12. Do a SWOT analysis – regularly.

CASE STUDIES

Peter grasps the nettle

Peter has never been self-employed before. He has been an employee of a large superstore chain in the DIY trade. He believes that there is a gap in the market in his town for a well-run hardware/DIY shop. He takes advice, researches the availability of shops, and when he finds one, he takes the plunge.

He believes he has learned the basics of the trade, and knows the main suppliers of goods to sell. He believes he has some good ideas for special promotions to get the shop off to a good start. His wife shares his vision, and works with him in the shop. However, they need other part-time help at certain times of the week and have to take on staff. He gets the professional help he needs, so that he goes about things in the right way.

The one thing he had not reckoned on is the dramatic change in lifestyle, from being an employee to being self-employed, and becoming an employer. He has to learn the vital skills of self-management and time management. This comes gradually with experience, but he finds that the learning curve is steep.

POINTS TO CONSIDER

1. How can you obtain the necessary skills to manage yourself, your time and other people?
2. Have you made an inventory of all the equipment you need?

3. Do you think your equipment needs will increase as your business expands?

4. Are your business prospects hampered by your premises?

5. Is your business computerised? Does it need to be?

6. Do you have the necessary skills to be an employer?

9

Complying with Regulations

One of the biggest gripes of self-employed people is the amount of red tape which hinders their work. The burden of regulation often hampers the way they can carry on business, and they resent having to act as unpaid tax collectors for the government. However, laws and regulations are a fact of life. They exist to protect:

- consumers
- employees
- yourself.

PAYING INCOME TAX

Taxes are the price we pay for a civilised society. We all have to pay our fair share, whether employed or self-employed. However, you need to know how to comply with the special requirements if you are self-employed.

The self assessment system has been with us for a few years now. Here is a brief summary of self assessment as it affects self-employed people.

Getting a tax return

If you have not filled in a tax return before, and you have a source of income that is not taxed at source, you must notify the Inland Revenue by 5 October following the end of the tax year in which you received that source of income.

(The tax year runs from 6 April to the following 5 April.) If you have sent in a tax return before, then you should receive a tax return shortly after 5 April each year. If you do not receive a tax return, and you continue to receive income liable to tax, then you must notify the Inland Revenue, by 5 October following the end of the tax year.

It is best to notify the Inland Revenue when you first become self-employed. They will then send you a notification form (see Figure 4). This is used by them for registering you as a self-employed person, and it is also used for National Insurance contribution purposes, and for VAT purposes, although it is not a VAT registration form. You have to apply for that separately.

Keeping records

The law requires you to keep such records as are needed to allow you to make a complete and correct tax return. For self-employed people, this specifically includes records of:

- all amounts received and spent in the business, and a description of the receipts and expenses

- all sales and purchases of goods in the trade (where the business involves trading in goods).

The legal requirements are obviously not a complete guide to what you need to keep to provide an adequate record of your business transactions. Although not a legal requirement it is a good idea to have a separate bank account for the business. Chapter 11 looks in more detail at bookkeeping, administration and filing.

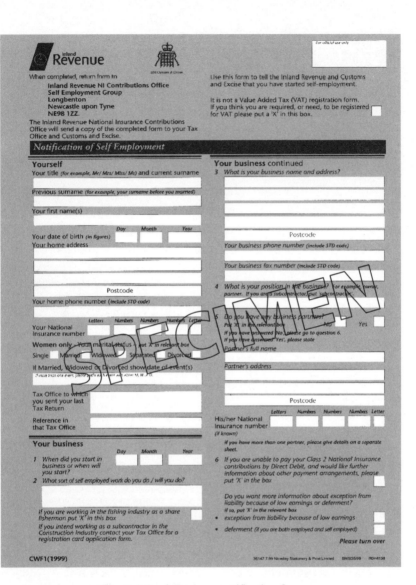

Fig. 4. Inland Revenue notification form.

Your business continued

7 Do you employ anybody, including members of your family, to work in your business?

Put 'X' in the relevant box No ☐ Yes ☐

If you have answered 'No', please go to question 8.
If you have answered 'Yes', read the statements below and put 'X' in the boxes that apply to your employees.

I have employees who earn

- £66 a week or £286 a month or more but less than £83 a week or £361 a month ☐
- £83 a week or £361 a month or more ☐
- more than £1 a week and have other employment ☐

8 If you took over an existing business, what was the name and address of the person you acquired it from?

```
[                                    ]
[                                    ]
[                                    ]
[           Postcode                 ]
```

9 If you are, or will be, doing all your work for one person or firm, state their name and address

```
[                                    ]
[                                    ]
[           Postcode                 ]
```

Your previous employment

10 What were you doing before you started this self employment? If you were unemployed, please state what you were doing before you became unemployed. Put 'X' in the relevant box below.

I was employed – give your employer's name and address below, the date the employment ended, and go to 11. ☐

I was self employed – give your business name and address below, the date the business ceased trading and go to 12. ☐

I was in full time education – give the date the education finished and go to 13. ☐

Name and address of employer/business

```
[                                    ]
[                                    ]
[                                    ]
[           Postcode                 ]
```

	Day	Month	Year
Date employment/ business/education ended			

11 If you were employed and you have a leaving certificate form P45 from your last employer
- keep Part 1A
- attach Parts 2 and 3 to this form and put 'X' in this box to show that you have done so.

Tax Returns

To make sure that we send you a Tax Return suited to your needs under Self Assessment, please answer these questions.

12 Do you have, in addition to the self employment described on this form, any other paid employment or an existing business which you will continue to run?

Put 'X' in the relevant box No ☐ Yes ☐

If you have answered 'No', please go to question 13.
If you have answered 'Yes', please put 'X' in the box(es) that apply to you.

- I am in paid employment as well as being self employed ☐
- I have an existing business as well as this self employment ☐

Name and address of employer/existing business

```
[                                    ]
[                                    ]
[           Postcode                 ]
```

13 Do you have an agent to advise you on your tax affairs?

Put 'X' in the relevant box No ☐ Yes ☐

If you have answered 'No', please go to the Declaration below.
If you have answered 'Yes', please enter details below.

Agent's name and address

```
[                                    ]
[                                    ]
[           Postcode                 ]
```

Agent's phone number (include STD code)

Have you completed form 64-8 (Agent authorisation)?

Yes ☐ No ☐

Declaration

This is my notification of self employment and I have given details of my business on this form.

I understand and agree that the information on this form will be made available to the Inland Revenue and Customs and Excise.

Signed [   ]

	Day	Month	Year
Date (in figures)			

Now you have completed the form, please return it to the Inland Revenue National Insurance Contributions Office at the address shown on the front of this form.

Fig. 4. continued.

National Insurance contributions

Application to pay Class 2 contributions by Direct Debit

FOR OFFICIAL USE ONLY
1st request from bank
CA2347 issued

QB started

DN
Start date - a Sunday

LO Serial number

1. Date self-employment started

2. Would you like us to collect contributions due from the start of your self-employment with the first Direct Debit payment? Yes ☐ No ☐

3. National Insurance number
Letters Numbers Letter

4. Surname and first two initials

5. Title (ie, Mr, Mrs, Miss, Ms)

6. Date of birth   1 9

7. Address
Postcode #

8. Daytime telephone number (including the STD code)
STD code Telephone number

9. Your Bank/Building Society sort code

10. Your Bank or Building Society account number

11. Name(s) of account holder(s)

12. Class of contribution
2

13. What sort of self-employed work do you do/will you do?

14. The name of your business

15. The address of your business. Fill this in even if your home and business address are the same
Postcode #

CA5601

Revenue National Insurance Contributions Office, Self Employment Group Application Processing Centre, Longbenton, Newcastle upon Tyne, NE98 1ZZ

Name(s) of account holder(s)

Bank/Building Society account number

Branch Sort Code

Name and address of Bank/Building Society branch
To: The Manager   Bank/Building Society
Address
Postcode

Instruction to your Bank or Building Society to pay by Direct Debits.

DIRECT Debit

Originator's Identification Number
9 9 1 1 3 3

Reference Number (National Insurance number)

Instruction to your Bank or Building Society.
Please pay Inland Revenue National Insurance Contributions Office Direct Debits from the account detailed in this Instruction subject to the safeguards assured by The Direct Debit Guarantee. I understand that this Instruction may remain with the Inland Revenue National Insurance Contributions Office and, if so, details will be passed electronically to my Bank/Building Society.

Signature(s)

Date

Some Banks or Building Societies may not accept Direct Debit Instructions for some types of account

Fig. 4. continued.

About Direct Debit

How to apply to pay by Direct Debit

If you are newly self-employed you must fill in form CWF 1 - "Notification of self-employment" in addition to this application form.

You **must** return **both** forms to the Inland Revenue National Insurance Contributions Office.

We regret that the facility to pay by Direct Debit is not available to share fishermen. Our leaflet CA11 "National Insurance for share fishermen" gives more information.

How will payments be made?

The application form asks you if you wish to pay by Direct Debit from the start of your self-employment. In most cases this means that all contributions due from the start of your self-employment will be collected with the first payment from your Bank or Building Society.

If you do not wish to pay by Direct Debit from the start of your self-employment **or we cannot arrange this, your Direct Debit will be started from a current date. We will then send you a separate bill for any contributions due from the start of your self-employment to the date your Direct Debit begins.**

Although we act at once to set up your Direct Debit, it may take some weeks before the first National Insurance contributions are collected from your account. We will write to tell you when the first payment will be made. Please ensure that you have enough funds in your account to meet your first payment.

After that payments:

- will be made automatically for as long as you wish

and

- will normally be deducted from your account on the second Friday of each month

These payments will cover National Insurance contributions for either four or five weeks, depending on the number of Sundays in the preceding tax month. The tax month ends on the 5th of each month.

A regular check of your Bank/Building Society statements will reassure you that payments have been made correctly.

What happens if you are ill?

You do not have to pay National Insurance contributions for any complete week (Sunday to Saturday) of illness. If you want to be credited with National Insurance contributions for these weeks you must provide evidence of your illness to your local Social Security office (in Northern Ireland send in sick notes to Incapacity Benefits Branch, Castle Court, Royal Avenue, Belfast BT1 1SB). We will reduce your Direct Debit payments to take into account full weeks of sickness as quickly as possible. You must still pay National Insurance contributions for any part weeks of illness. If you do claim Incapacity Benefit credits your local Benefits Agency (in Northern Ireland send in sick notes to Incapacity Benefits Branch, Castle Court, Royal Avenue, Belfast BT1 1SB) will advise us when your period of incapacity ends. If your Direct Debit payments do not restart, please let us know immediately.

What to do if you change Bank or Building Society

You should tell us if you change your Bank or Building Society. You will have to fill in another Direct Debit application form as Direct Debits cannot be transferred between Banks or Building Societies. However, this may not be necessary if you are only changing branches of the same Bank or Building Society.

Direct Debit Application

The Direct Debit Guarantee

This guarantee is offered by all Banks and Building Societies that take part in the Direct Debit Scheme. The efficiency and security of the Scheme is monitored and protected by your own Bank or Building Society.

If the amounts to be paid or the payment dates change, the Inland Revenue National Insurance Contributions Office will notify you 10 working days in advance of your account being debited or as otherwise agreed.

If an error is made by the Inland Revenue National Insurance Contributions Office or your Bank or Building Society, you are guaranteed a full and immediate refund from your branch of the amount paid.

You can cancel a Direct Debit at any time by writing to your Bank or Building Society. Please also send a copy of your letter to us.

Inland Revenue National Insurance Contributions Office

Self Employment Group

Customer Account Section

Longbenton

Newcastle upon Tyne

NE98 1ZZ

Fig. 4. continued.

Self-employed people must retain their accounting records for five years from the latest date for filing your tax return which includes the business accounts concerned. There are penalties for not producing adequate records if required by the Inland Revenue, and for failing to retain them for the required period.

Filling in the tax return

When you get your tax return, it consists of the 'core' return, plus any additional pages which the Inspector of Taxes thinks you need. Additional pages relate to different sources of income, such as employment income, self-employment income, partnership income, income from abroad, etc.

First, make sure you have all the pages you need. If you have a source of income, but you do not have the correct pages, phone the order line for them.

Next, collect together all the information concerning the income from all your sources, and all the claims for allowances and reliefs. Then go through the return and additional pages, filling in all the details of your income and claims. There is a guide booklet which comes with the tax return, and gives you advice about how to fill in the boxes.

When you have filled in the boxes, decide whether you want to calculate the tax yourself or get the Inland Revenue to calculate it. You may ask the Inland Revenue to calculate the tax only if you send the return back by 30 September following the end of the tax year. If you send it in after that date, or if you choose to calculate your own tax, there is a tax calculation guide. Work your way through this, and enter the tax payable in the appropriate box in the tax return.

Finally, sign the tax return where indicated. This confirms that you certify that the tax return is correct and complete. Then post it off to the Inland Revenue. It must reach them by 31 January following the tax year at the very latest.

Paying the tax

The onus is on you to calculate your own tax and pay it when it becomes due. In practice, however, the Inland Revenue send you a statement of account shortly before your payments become due. The tax is payable as follows:

- The balance of tax for the previous year is payable by 31 January following the end of the tax year.

- The first instalment of tax on account for the next year is also payable on 31 January.

- The second instalment of tax on account for the next year is payable the following 31 July.

Payments on account

The payments on account for one year are calculated by reference to the actual tax paid for the previous year. If you think your tax bill should be reduced for the next year, you may apply to reduce the payments on account. However, if you pay too little on account, you will have to pay interest on any short payments, from the due date.

If the payments on account are more than the final tax liability for the year, the Inland Revenue will refund the overpayment to you, or deduct it from the next payment due.

Avoiding penalties, interest and surcharges

The Inland Revenue have the power to impose penalties, although they can mitigate the penalties if they see good reason:

Late delivery of tax return	Penalty £100 if it is up to six months late
	Penalty £200 if more than six months late up to one year late
	Penalty up to 100% of tax due if over one year late
Delay after the Commissioners direct that you must send in a tax return	£60 per day
Failure to keep and retain proper records	Up to £3,000 for each failure
Failure to produce records requested by Inspector of Taxes in the course of an enquiry	£50, plus £30 per day

Interest is charged on all late payments on a daily basis at the official rate, which is published by the Inland Revenue from time to time. They emphasise that this is in no way a penalty, but is merely designed to provide commercial restitution for the use of the money. If the Inland Revenue are late in paying you, they will also pay you interest at the same official rate.

Surcharges are added to tax payable if you pay late. If tax is paid more than 28 days late, up to six months late, the surcharge is 5% of the tax due. If tax is paid more than six months late, the surcharge is 10% of the tax due.

Adjustments and enquiries

Correcting mistakes
If you discover that you have made an error in your tax return, you may amend the tax return by writing to the Inspector of Taxes at any time up to one year from the normal filing date. The Inspector of Taxes may correct any 'manifest mistake' in your tax return within nine months of receiving your tax return, and he must notify you of the corrections.

Enquiries by the Inspector of Taxes
As part of the verification procedure, the Inland Revenue pick out a small number of tax returns at random. These are then subject to enquiry by the Inspector of Taxes. They may also enquire into any tax return if there is an aspect of the figures which they believe requires further investigation.

The Inspector of Taxes does not have to justify any enquiry into your tax return, and you must be ready to provide any information and explanation required.

PAYING VALUE ADDED TAX

Value Added Tax was conceived as a simple tax. A flat rate of tax was to be added to all 'outputs' of a business, and paid over to the Commissioners of Customs and Excise. In fact, there are now three different rates of tax, and it is anything but a simple tax.

The principle is that a registered business adds VAT to its sales (the outputs tax). If it receives supplies of goods or services from another registered business, there will be VAT added to that price. This is its inputs tax. The business offsets its inputs tax against its outputs tax, and pays over the difference. Usually, a business will have more outputs tax that inputs tax, and therefore has to pay over the difference to Customs and Excise. Sometimes, however, the inputs tax will exceed the outputs tax, and the difference is refunded by Customs and Excise.

Registering for VAT

A business must register for VAT if its turnover for any twelve consecutive months is above the registration limit. This limit is announced each year in the budget. At the time of writing it is £56,000. When you are in business, therefore, you have an obligation to keep proper records of your turnover, whether you are VAT registered or not.

When you reach the limit, you have 30 days to notify the Customs and Excise. They will require you to complete a VAT registration form (see Figure 5). You are registered from the beginning of the following month.

You may also register voluntarily. There are certain circumstances when this is advantageous to you – mainly when you have zero rated sales.

Deregistering from VAT

If you are registered for VAT, you may deregister if your turnover for any twelve consecutive months falls below the deregistration limit. This limit is announced each year in the budget, and is usually a couple of thousand pounds below the registration limit. At the time of writing, it is £54,000.

Filling in the VAT returns

When you are registered, you must fill in returns. These normally cover three months, but if you normally receive a repayment, you may opt to have monthly returns. There is also the option to do 'annual accounting' for VAT, in which case the return is yearly.

The VAT return shows the outputs tax, the inputs tax, and the difference between them, being the amount you owe to Customs and Excise or the amount they owe you. The form also has boxes for other statistics. It must be sent to Customs and Excise within a month of the return date.

Avoiding the penalties and interest
Like the Inland Revenue, the Customs and Excise have power to impose penalties. Here are the main penalties:

Failure to register	£50 plus	– 5% of the tax lost if the failure does not exceed nine months
		– 10% of the tax lost if the failure exceeds nine months but not eighteen months
		– 15% of the tax lost if the failure exceeds eighteen months
Issuing an invoice purporting to show VAT when you are not registered	£50 plus	– 15% of the amount of VAT falsely shown

Part 1 About the business

Name

1 **Sole proprietors** – please give your full name.

Partnerships – please give your trading name, or if you do not have one please give the names of all partners. You must also complete and return form VAT 2 (available from the National Advice Service or our website).

Corporate or unincorporated bodies – please give the name of the company, club, association, etc.

2 **Do you have a trading name?** (Please tick)   ☐ Yes   ☐ No

Please give the trading name of the business.

Status

3 **What is the structure/legal status of the business?** (Please tick)

☐ Sole proprietor   ☐ Partnership (Please complete form VAT 2)

☐ Corporate body (e.g. limited company)

Please give incorporation details   Certificate no.

Date of incorporation

Country of incorporation

☐ Unincorporated body (e.g. club or association)

Please specify

Business address

4 **Please give the address of your principal place of business. This is where you carry out most of the day-to-day running of the business.** e.g. where you receive and deal with orders.

Postcode

Business phone

Fax number

Mobile phone

E-mail address

Internet address

SPECIMEN

Page 1

Fig. 5. VAT registration form.
(pages 1, 2 and 3 of 7)

96

Business activities

5 Please tell us about all your current and/or intended business activities.
(Continue on a separate sheet if necessary)

6 Are you or any of the partners or directors in the business you are seeking to register through this application, involved in running any other businesses either as a sole proprietor, partner or director? (Please tick)

☐ Yes ☐ No

If **yes**, please give the names of these businesses and VAT registration numbers where appropriate.
(Continue on a separate sheet if necessary)

7 Have you, or any of the partners or directors in the business you are seeking to register through this application, been involved in running any other businesses either as a sole proprietor, partner or director in the past two years? (Please tick)

☐ Yes ☐ No

If **yes**, please give the names of these businesses and VAT registration numbers where appropriate.
(Continue on a separate sheet if necessary)

8 Is your business involved in any other activities registered with or authorised by Customs and Excise? (Please tick boxes as appropriate)

☐ Excise duties ☐ Imports/exports
☐ Landfill tax ☐ Air passenger duty
☐ Insurance premium tax ☐ Climate change levy
☐ Aggregates levy (From 1/4/2002)

9 Are you registering as the representative member of a VAT group? (Please tick)

☐ Yes ☐ No

If **yes**, you must provide the additional information set out on forms VAT 50 and VAT 51 (available from the National Advice Service tel: 0845 010 9000 or our website).

Part 2 About the business accounts

VAT returns

10 Do you expect to receive regular repayments of VAT? (Please tick)

☐ Yes ☐ No

Do not answer **yes** if you believe that the majority of your VAT returns will show an overall payment of tax due to Customs and Excise.

Page 2

Fig. 5. continued.

97

Computer accounts

11 Is your accounting system computerised?
(Please tick)

☐ Yes   ☐ No

If **yes**, please give details of the software used in compiling your accounts.

Software
[   ]

Version
[   ]

Bank details

12 Please give details of the bank or building society account that you use for the business.

Sort code
[| |]

Account number
[| | | |]

or Girobank account number
[| | | | | |]

Part 3 The taxable turnover and date of registration

Start of business

For the purposes of VAT, all the goods or services you supply which are VAT-rated – even zero-rated goods or services – are called 'taxable supplies', whether you are registered for VAT or not. The purchases you make for your business are not your taxable supplies.

13 Have you made any taxable supplies yet?
(Please tick)

☐ Yes   ☐ No

If **yes**, give the date of your first taxable supply.
If **no**, give the date you expect it to be.

Date of first taxable supply
[| | | | |]

Business transfers

14 Have you taken over a VAT registered business from someone else as a going concern, or changed the legal entity that owns the business (for example from a sole proprietor to a limited company)? (Please tick)

☐ Yes   ☐ No (If no proceed to question 18)

If **yes**, what date did the transfer of the business or change in legal entity take place?

[| | | | |]

15 Who was the previous owner?

[   ]

16 What was their VAT number?

[| | | |]

17 Do you want to keep this number? (Please tick)

☐ Yes   ☐ No

If **yes**, you and the previous owner must also complete and return form VAT 68 (available from the National Advice Service tel 0845 010 9000 or our website). If you do keep the VAT number, remember that you will become liable for the previous owner's VAT debts.

Page 3

Fig. 5. continued.

Default surcharge	£30 plus	– 2% of VAT due for first default
for late return		– 5% of VAT due for second default
		– 10% of VAT due for third default
		– 15% of VAT due for fourth and subsequent defaults
Misdeclaration and Persistent Misdeclaration found by Customs and Excise		15% of tax lost if misdeclaration had not been found

Like the Inland Revenue, Customs and Excise charge interest at their official rate (not the same as the Inland Revenue rate) on tax paid late.

PAYING PAYE

If you have any employees working for you, you must operate a PAYE system. This is the means by which you, the employer, collect income tax and National Insurance from the employee on behalf of the Inland Revenue, and then pay it over to the Inland Revenue. The system is also used to pay statutory sick pay, statutory maternity pay, working families tax credit, and to collect repayments of student loans.

The system is operated by paperwork which the Inland Revenue supply. They also carry out training on operating the PAYE system, by having occasional 'workshops'. However, the paperwork for operating the PAYE system does come with a complete guide, and you can learn the system by reading it. Many self-employed people however, seek the help and advice of their accountant either to operate the system for them, or to get them started.

It is important to get it right. Although you act as an unpaid tax collector for the government, there are penalties for not sending in the paperwork on time, and especially for not paying over the money deducted from employees.

PAYING NATIONAL INSURANCE

As a self-employed person, you are liable to pay class 2 contributions. These are not onerous – at the time of writing only £2 per week. However, the onus is on you to pay. It is not deducted automatically. Collection of National Insurance is now in the hands of the Inland Revenue, and they send you a bill every three months.

You are also liable to Class 4 National Insurance. This is levied at a fixed percentage (which is set once a year) on your self-employed profits up to a certain maximum. The calculation of this is done on your self assessment tax return, and the payment is made together with your income tax payment.

ENSURING HEALTH AND SAFETY AT WORK

There are a number of laws and regulations governing the issue of health and safety at work. The most important is the **Health and Safety at Work etc. Act 1974** but other important Acts and regulations are:

- Factories Act 1961
- Offices Shops and Railway Premises Act 1963
- Fire Precautions Act 1971

- Food Safety Act 1990
- Food Labelling Regulations 1996.

Under these Acts, there are inspectors who can arrive unannounced to inspect your premises, and they have the power to issue 'Improvement Notices' giving you at least 21 days' notice to improve your practices. They also have the power to issue 'Prohibition Notices' ordering you to stop doing something if they judge it to be dangerous to you, your employees, or the public. The Health and Safety Commission issue numerous booklets and guides covering numerous subjects. If you think there may be particular safety or health risks in your business, you can probably find a booklet or guide about it.

If you have five or more employees, you must have, and display, a written health and safety policy. You must also have a nominated first aid officer, and someone who carries out regular health and safety risk assessments, which must be recorded and kept.

Special licences are required for anyone who handles:

- asbestos
- acetylene
- explosives
- nuclear installations
- petroleum products.

There are provisions covering many areas. The following is not an exhaustive list, but it indicates the sort of issues of which you must be aware:

- display screen equipment (such as computer screens) – employers must pay for staff to have regular eye tests
- electricity at work
- employers' liability
- fire precautions
- first aid at work
- health surveillance
- manual handling
- noise at work
- personal protective equipment
- recording and reporting of accidents, injuries and illnesses at work
- safety signs (e.g. prohibiting entry, fire escapes, etc.)
- work equipment
- work places (including rest rooms, canteens, toilets, changing rooms, etc.)
- waste products – this even covers waste paper from the office
- young persons.

CONSUMER LAW

Your general dealings when working for yourself are governed by contract law. Although you may not sign many written contracts, most of your dealings give rise to implied contracts. It is not within the scope of this book to cover contract law fully, but if you find yourself in difficulties, you will probably need to consult a solicitor.

A consumer has more protection at law than another business, since a consumer is assumed to be less commercially knowledgeable than a business person. There are various implied terms when you sell your goods or services to a consumer.

For a sale of goods:

- The person transferring the goods must have the right to do so.
- The goods must correspond to any description given.
- The goods must be of satisfactory quality.
- The goods must be fit for the purpose intended.

For a sale of services:

- The services must be supplied with reasonable care.
- The services must be provided with reasonable display of the skills the person purports to have in offering the service.
- The services must be performed within a reasonable time.
- The services must be performed at a reasonable price.

Looking at these implied terms, it is obvious that a lot will depend on the definition of 'reasonable' in the circumstances of each case. There are some definitions in the laws, but there is still much that could be subject to dispute. What you cannot do, however, is to include unreasonable or unfair terms which limit or exclude your liability under these implied terms.

Here are some of the main Acts and regulations:

- Competition Act 1998
- Consumer Protection Act 1987
- Consumer Credit Act 1974
- Data Protection Act 1998

- Sale of Goods Act 1979
- Sunday Trading Act 1994
- Supply of Goods and Services Act 1982
- Trade Descriptions Act 1968
- Trade Marks Act 1994.

CHECKLIST

Make sure you:

- pay your income tax
- pay your National Insurance contributions
- register for VAT when necessary
- pay your VAT
- pay PAYE when you have employees
- keep your workplace safe and assess any safety or health risks
- comply with consumer protection legislation.

CASE STUDIES

Neil takes on an assistant and expands his business

Neil has started a dry cleaning business. The shop has done well, and he is starting to find more work in carpet cleaning and soft furniture cleaning on location. To develop this side of the business, he takes on an employee to keep the shop going while he goes out to do work at other locations.

He has to set up a PAYE system, and ensure that he obtains a P45 from the employee he takes on. He tries to follow the instructions, but finds difficulty in implementing it. He therefore calls upon his accountant to help him out, by showing him what to do. Once he has been shown, he takes over the responsibility, with the promise of more help if there are any complications such as sick pay, etc.

As his business is expanding, he has to register for VAT, and again he has to use his accountant's help in registering, setting up accounting systems, and completing his first return and paying the VAT due.

POINTS TO CONSIDER

1. Do you know which areas of your business are governed by laws and regulations?

2. Are you able to identify what you need to comply with laws and regulations, or do you need to ask a professional?

10

Financing Your Operation

KNOWING WHAT YOU NEED

So here you are at the start of a great new venture – you are becoming self-employed. You have a great idea, and a bit of a nest egg from your redundancy money. But have you got enough money? If not, how can you get enough money to get you started? And then what about the future – will you need to borrow again?

The first thing to do is to make out a list of all the items of equipment, property, vehicles, etc. you need. Just put the absolutely essential items in this list. Things that would be nice but are not essential can be left until later. Then do as much work as you can on putting prices on the items – either new or second-hand. This gives you the total you need to spend.

Chapter 4 dealt with managing working capital, and producing a cash flow forecast. The finance for your fixed assets – equipment, property, vehicles, etc. – is a different sort of finance.

REVIEWING THE OPTIONS

There are several options for getting finance. As we have seen, finance for working capital is a different animal from finance for fixed assets.

You would expect fixed assets to have a definite life span. In the normal course of events, you would expect that life to be counted in years, rather than months or weeks. Working capital, on the other hand, changes from one day to the next – even from one hour to the next.

The general principle is this:

> **Match the finance to the life of the asset as far as possible.**

Thus, the normal way to finance working capital is by an overdraft. This is a facility for your bank account to go 'into the red'. Because of the nature of working capital, the amount by which you are 'in the red' will fluctuate from day to day. Interest is only charged on the actual amount by which you are 'in the red', and it is charged on a daily basis. This is therefore the most economical way to finance your working capital, and also one that gives you a regular monitor of the way your working capital is behaving.

There are a number of options to finance your fixed assets:

- mortgages
- loans
- hire purchase
- leasing
- equity finance.

MORTGAGES
This is the usual way of financing the purchase of property

– particularly if you buy it freehold. In this case, you would expect to own it indefinitely, or at least for as long as it suits your requirements. A mortgage loan is therefore usually given for anything up to about 25 years – depending on your age.

The principle of a mortgage is that the person or company that loans you the money (the mortgagor) has a title to the property. That means that if you cannot keep up the repayments, the mortgagor has the right to repossess the property, and sell it to recoup the money outstanding.

Many banks and building societies offer mortgages on commercial property, although some restrict their borrowing to residential property only. There are other commercial mortgage companies in this market. You may also think about going to a commercial mortgage broker. These are independent brokers with wide experience of getting commercial loans and mortgages. They can often negotiate better terms and interest rates for you, which will more than offset any fee they charge.

LOANS

You may be able to get a private loan from a friend or family member. If so, remember that this is still a commercial transaction. Get an agreement drawn up to cover interest, repayments, etc. Disputes about money can sour even the best relationships, so make sure that both parties – the lender and the borrower – agree what the terms are, and just what the liabilities are.

Secured loans

It is more common to get a loan from a bank. Loans may be **secured or unsecured**. A secured loan is the same in this respect as a mortgage. The lender takes a legal charge on some property, and if you are unable to repay, the lender can force a sale of the property. The property is not necessarily the same as the item on which the loan is given. For example, you could get a loan to buy machinery, but it is secured on your own home. Loans secured on your own home represent a further degree of risk, which you must weigh up very carefully before committing yourself.

A legal charge on a property may be a **first charge or a second charge**. A first charge means that there is no other person or company with a prior legal charge over the property. A second charge means that there is someone else with a first charge. The lender's security is therefore relegated to a second position. If the worst were to happen, the property would be sold, and the proceeds would go first to repay the lender with the first charge. Only if there was something left over would the person with the second charge get their money. In theory, it is also possible to have a third or fourth charge, or even more. In practice, however, it is rare to see more than a second charge.

A lender who has to take a second charge will therefore do two things:

♦ They will get a valuation of the property, and find out the amount of the first charge, to see if there is enough value in the property to support their second charge. You, the borrower, would have to pay for this valuation.

- They will charge more for the loan to cover the increased risk of taking a second charge.

Unsecured loans

Banks may also consider giving a loan without security. This obviously represents a higher risk for them, so the interest and charges will be higher. Normally this sort of loan is for smaller amounts than secured loans, and for some item of identifiable equipment, machinery, vehicle, etc. The bank may well ask to see regular accounts showing the progress of your business if they grant a loan, particularly if they are granting you an overdraft as well.

Often, if an unsecured loan is not possible, the bank will look for a personal guarantee against you.

DEALING WITH YOUR BANK

One of the best ways of dealing with your bank is to find one that you can work with, and build up a relationship over a number of years. If you have had a bank account while employed, then go self-employed, try to use the same bank – do not necessarily switch to another bank (unless they are totally uncooperative, of course).

If you intend to make a success of your business, building up a good relationship with your bank can be invaluable. They will be sympathetic when you need help. Of course, you cannot guarantee that the same manager will be there all the time – especially in these days when banks are going all out to cut costs by cutting jobs. But even if the manager changes, they will have a file which shows the sort of customer you have been.

Negotiating the loan

The terms are not fixed in concrete. Part of the overall negotiation with a bank consists of agreeing their charges and the interest, and the repayment term. Try to keep the repayment term within the expected life of the asset. This is for your benefit as well as the bank's.

The facilities granted to you by the bank will be reviewed regularly. Be prepared to renegotiate the terms when it comes up for review. The bank will expect you to negotiate – you are, after all, operating commercially as much as they are.

Here are some tips for negotiating a loan or facility:

♦ Ask for at least 10% more than you need.

♦ Ask for at least 25% longer to repay than you need.

♦ Do not agree to too much security. Work out the bank's maximum exposure to loss, and agree to that much. If they ask for double that amount, it is too much.

♦ Try to avoid having to give a personal guarantee – the bigger your business, the more likely this is.

♦ Start with getting acceptance of the proposal – leave negotiation of rates until the end.

◆ Get the bank to confirm all terms in writing, and get copies of all agreements you have signed.

Maintaining good relationships

Here are some tips for maintaining a good working relationship with your bank manager.

Keep to agreements made

Make sure that you can make repayments when they are due. Do not infringe your overdraft limit. The bank can refuse payment of cheques. This will result in a charge on your account, and could damage your reputation with the person you issued the cheque to.

Forewarn the bank of infringements

Sometimes you are unavoidably going to go over your bank overdraft limit. If you know this is going to happen, tell the bank as soon as you can. Be as precise as you can – tell them how much you are going over your limit, and how long it will last. The bank is unlikely to refuse this request, and they will not then bounce any cheques.

Mollify the bank when there's bad news

If you have to tell the bank that something has gone wrong, always show what action you are taking to remedy the situation.

Demonstrate your awareness

In all your dealings with the bank, try to show that you are commercially aware, that you are up to date with your own business's transactions, and that you can control your businesses's finances.

Never rush the bank for a decision
They have their own timetable, and will not delay you unnecessarily.

Do not tell the bank you are shopping around
The bank is looking for a long-term relationship just as much as you are. Therefore, do not try to use the 'shopping around' technique as a negotiating ploy. However, it is useful to know what the going rate is for charges and interest.

Think ahead
The successful end of one negotiation is the end of that chapter, not the end of the story. Look ahead to your future development, and start preparing the way for the next negotiations with your bank.

The essentials
When dealing with your bank, you have to persuade them to lend the money to you. The most important things are:

◆ Tell them why you need the finance. You cannot just say that you need more money. That is too vague. Give a specific purpose for the money you need.

◆ Tell them how much you need. Demonstrate that it is realistic compared to your own stake in the business.

◆ Demonstrate that you have the ability to repay the money.

◆ Show them that you have thought about problem areas – what if something goes wrong?

◆ Show who is in control – demonstrate that you are driving the business.

HIRE PURCHASE

This is a well-known form of finance. It consists of a legal agreement by which the hire purchase company becomes the legal owner of the goods. There is a separate agreement for each item of goods covered. You pay them a deposit and regular (usually monthly) repayments. The repayments include interest as well as the price of the goods. If you default on the repayments, they can repossess the goods. When you have paid off the last instalment, the goods are legally yours.

The interest rate for hire purchase transactions is usually higher than a straightforward bank loan.

LEASING

There are two types of leasing – **operating leases and purchase leases**. Purchase leases are in essence virtually the same as hire purchase agreements.

Operating leases can apply to property or other moveable assets.

Property leases (renting)

Renting a commercial property can be a viable alternative to buying. You will be presented with a lease to sign. Get this checked by an estate agent you trust, or a solicitor. Check out the things listed in Chapter 8.

Operating leases

This form of lease is often used for financing equipment or vehicles. You pay a monthly or quarterly rent for the use of the item, and this is an expense of your business, on which you can reclaim the VAT (an argument often used by leasing companies). At the end of the term of the lease, there is sometimes an 'Option Payment'. This is a settlement figure which you can pay, and the goods become yours. There may also be an extension clause, by which you may extend the term of the lease, usually for a reduced leasing charge.

Each lease agreement is different, and you need to check the terms carefully. Although it is an operating lease, the amount of the regular payments is usually calculated by reference to the cost of the goods and an interest charge. The interest charge inherent in an operating lease is usually higher than a bank loan.

EQUITY FINANCE

This is a form of finance in which the person supplying the finance does not lend you the money. He or she actually becomes a part owner of the business. An equity partner may be one who actively participates, or not.

If your business is in the form of a limited company, the provider of equity finance buys a number of shares, and is therefore a part owner of the company. They may not necessarily be a director, and if not, they do not take part in the running of the company. If your business is a limited company, and you seek equity finance, look for answers to the following questions:

◆ How many shares will the equity partner have – more than you?
◆ Will the equity partner participate in the running of the company?

- What reward does the equity partner want?
- Is it appropriate to issue shares of a different class for the equity partner?
- Will the equity partner have full voting rights?

If your business is a one man band, an equity partner would come in as a partner in the business. Again, it is very important to agree exactly the terms on which the equity partner comes in.

Whatever form the equity partnership takes, the key element is that the equity partner is a part owner of the business, sharing in some way in the risks and the profit. Make sure that the agreement covers all eventualities, including what happens if you make a loss, what would happen if the business should cease, etc.

Business angels

This is a form of finance which includes practical help of some sort. The business angel is a person with relevant business experience, often having taken early retirement, who will invest both some money and some time in your business. They bring their experience to help you, and put some money into your business, in the form of either loans or equity of some sort.

They have to satisfy themselves that yours is a viable business, and you have to satisfy yourself that you will be able to work with them.

MANAGING YOUR CASH FLOW

Chapter 4 dealt with your working capital, and forecasting it. Part of the business of providing finance for your working capital requirement is actively managing the cash flow. In practice this means managing your working capital. To recap, the elements of your working capital are:

◆ stock
◆ work in progress
◆ debtors
◆ expenses paid in advance
◆ creditors.

Each of these elements eventually translates into cash – the first four represent cash going into your bank, the last, cash going out. Therefore, you must manage all these items to ensure that you can keep within your bank overdraft facilities.

Stock

Make sure that you do not carry too much stock. The cost of carrying too much stock is seen in three ways:

◆ The cost of financing the stock itself.
◆ The risk of obsolescence, loss or damage.
◆ The cost of storage.

You will undoubtedly need to carry many different lines. Each of these must be controlled. Your business could suffer through being either understocked or overstocked. If you find any obsolete items, see if you can sell them off cheaply. If not, be prepared to write them off and learn from the experience.

If your business is retail or wholesale selling, this item is particularly important. Make sure you know which items are selling. If there are any lines which are not selling, find out why – is it something to do with the way they are displayed, the pricing, or general demand? If something is selling well, again try to find out why. It could just be that you have made a mistake in pricing, and are actually selling them at a loss.

If you are manufacturing, you need to know what quantities of raw materials you need, when you need them, and what the 'lead time' is (i.e. the delay between ordering stock and its delivery to you).

Whatever your business, set maximum and minimum levels of stock, and the lead time.

Work in progress
Try to keep this at a minimum at all times. If your business is particularly complicated, or you have many individual items of work in progress at any one time, active management is needed. Make sure that no items get overlooked and are lost in progress. Make sure that no deadlines or promised delivery dates are going to be breached.

Remember that time is money. As long as work is in progress and not completed, the money is not in your bank account.

Debtors
Once the goods have been sold, the money is still not in

your bank account. The customer becomes a debtor, and still has to pay you. There are several ways of managing your debtors.

Discounting

One way of encouraging customers to pay quickly is to add an amount on to all your prices, say 5% and state on your invoices 'Discount of 5% may be deducted if paid within . . . days.' Customers will of course realise that you have loaded this amount on the price in the first place. If they object, simply explain that you do not think it is fair that the customers who pay on time should be financing those who do not pay on time.

Interest

If your terms of business allow for it, you may charge interest on overdue accounts. The customer must be made aware of this. However, since the **Late Payment of Commercial Debts (Interest) Act 1998**, small firms have the legal right to charge interest to large firms who exceed their credit terms. Since November 2002, all firms are able to charge interest to any other firm.

Factoring

This is a service carried out by finance houses and banks. The factor 'buys' your debts from you, paying a high percentage up front, say 80%, and paying the rest when the debts are paid in full. For this, they charge a fee. They can also provide other services such as:

- taking over sales ledger administration
- assessing credit risks
- exporting assistance

- invoice discounting
- credit protection (this is known as 'non recourse', and the factor guarantees 100% protection against bad debts, for a further fee).

Invoice discounting

This is similar to factoring, but in this case, all that is supplied is the financing facility against invoices. A discount rate is applied, and you get that discounted amount of your invoices. Unlike factoring, there is no involvement with your sales ledger administration, and the customer does not know that your invoices are being discounted. Invoice discounting can be applied on a 'whole turnover' basis, or on a 'selected invoice' basis.

Credit control

Controlling your debtors is an important part of managing your cash flow. Perhaps confusingly, this is known generally as 'credit' control. You should exercise some form of control at all stages of the process of selling and collecting the debt.

- *Getting new customers* – try to get some credit reference to ensure that they are bona fide customers and that they have no adverse record.

- *Setting a credit limit* – set a debt limit above which they must not go. Make sure the customer knows the credit limit. It is up to you to monitor this; the customer will certainly not volunteer any breaches of the limit. If you are in doubt about the creditworthiness of a customer, you could ask for an advance payment, to ensure that the account is never in debt. Then, when the customer has traded with you for a period, you may relax this and allow a credit limit if you judge that the customer has acted responsibly.

♦ *Agreeing the terms of business* – give the customer written terms of business. There is then no dispute about the terms – in particular what period of credit is allowed.

♦ *Checking the debt* – make sure that before you supply any goods or services, the customer does not have a debt owing from a previous transaction, which has exceeded the payment terms.

♦ *Sending statements and reminders* – do not neglect to send statements of the amounts owing at regular intervals.

♦ *Chasing slow payers* – never let a debt go beyond its agreed term without chasing it. If letters get no response, try a telephone call. If there is still no response, a personal visit often works. Always remain polite, since certain actions can be judged to constitute harassment, which is an offence.

♦ *Sending an official letter* – a letter from a solicitor or debt collection agency often works when other methods have failed. This threatens that if payment is not made within a certain time, proceedings will be started for recovery in the County Court. A solicitor will charge a fixed fee for such a letter. Some debt collection agencies operate on a 'no collection, no fee' basis, and they follow through the procedures.

Legal proceedings

If all else fails, you will have to resort to legal action. This need not cost a lot of money. You can make a claim yourself under the rules for making small claims in the County Court. You submit a claim form to the County Court, for a judgement to be made against the debtor. The debtor then has a certain time to admit the claim, dispute it, or make a counter claim against you. If the debtor makes no response, a judgement is entered.

The judgement then has to be enforced, so that you can actually get the money owed. This also has to be done through the County Court. The options available are:

- *Execution against goods* – a bailiff will collect goods from the debtor to be sold at auction.

- *A charging order* – this is an order made on land or property owned by the debtor. This is similar to a mortgage debt secured on the property. If the debt is not paid, you can enforce the sale of the property to pay off the debt.

- *A garnishee order* – this is an order 'attaching' a debt owing to the debtor from a third party. This is often applied to a bank account. The account is frozen until the debt owing to you is paid.

- *Attachment of earnings* – this only applies where the debtor is employed. A regular amount will be deducted from the debtor's earnings and paid to you.

- *Bankruptcy or winding up* – this is a last resort measure. If there is no other means of collecting the debt, you can force the debtor into bankruptcy, or if the debtor is a company, into liquidation.

Creditors

Do not take excessive credit from your creditors – they supply the essential goods and services you need to operate. Make sure you know the terms of business with your creditors, and if you need extra time to pay in unusual circumstances, try to negotiate these individually.

CHECKLIST

1. Work out your needs.

2. Look at all the options.

3. Know how to manage your bank manger.

4. Actively manage your cash flow.

5. Control your debtors.

CASE STUDIES

Jane opens an antiques shop

Jane has had a lifelong interest in antiques, and is now embarking on self-employment by opening an antiques shop. She has received a small inheritance, which will help her on her way, but she needs more money. Her list of needs includes:

- shop premises
- decoration of the shop to create a good ambience
- enough stock to get started
- a few items of equipment
- a van.

She decides to get the van on hire purchase, get a small loan from the bank for the initial expenses and equipment, establish a relatively small overdraft for working capital, and rent the premises. She does not feel confident enough yet to buy the premises, but she manages to get a lease on premises in a good location for a period of six years, with the option to buy the premises at the end of that term.

David expands rapidly

David started in self-employment a few years ago, manufacturing a specialist product for the garden trade. He is good at invention and design, and he develops several new products. These prove so popular that he has to expand his operation rapidly.

This involves buying new factory premises, for which he gets a mortgage, taking on more employees, and generally increasing his working capital requirement. He works with his accountant to prepare a business plan for the next five years, which he takes to his bank, and agrees a new overdraft limit. He also factors his debts, to cope with the rapid expansion and the seasonal nature of the demand.

POINTS TO CONSIDER

1. Do you know what your requirements are for fixed assets, and for working capital?

2. Do you have adequate systems to allow you to control your working capital?

3. Are you able to control the money owing to you from debtors?

4. Do you feel that you get the right service from your bank manager?

Keeping Records

This is the boring bit! The one thing most self-employed people say is that they really want to get on with their job, and avoid the red tape. But some sort of record keeping is unavoidable, for your own sake as much as for anyone else's. Unless you have enough work to be able to pay someone else to do this, or you have a willing partner or spouse who will do the job, you just have to knuckle down to it.

BOOKKEEPING

This is the most obvious record keeping duty, and the one most people find difficult. There are usually evening classes in bookkeeping, if you want to learn to do a proper job yourself.

Tax requirements

The tax laws say that you must keep such records as are needed to make a complete and correct tax return each year. If you are self-employed, this specifically includes:

- all amounts received and spent in the business and a description of the receipts and expenses
- all sales and purchases of goods in the trade (where the business involves trading in goods).

In practice, the bare minimum is obviously not enough for you to keep an adequate record of your business. For instance, although the tax laws do not require it, a separate business bank account is a great benefit. Try to keep all your private transactions separate, and do this by having a private bank account and a business account.

Bookkeeping in detail

Your bookkeeping system should enable you to identify:

- all sales and other income of the business
- purchases of goods for resale
- overhead expenses
- purchases and sales of assets used in your business
- all amounts you take from the business, whether in the form of cash, cheque or goods in kind
- all amounts you put into the business from your personal sources
- private proportions of business expenses (such as motor expenses)
- values of stock and work in progress at the year end date.

The bare minimum

The exact type of bookkeeping system depends on the type of business. A bare minimum, common to all types of business, would include:

- cash book
- petty cash book.

If your business is small, with no credit sales, not registered for VAT, and no employees – such as a small retail shop – these could be all the books you need, apart from a stock-taking list each year. The receipts and payments would need to be analysed, and you can get cash books with analysis columns at any good commercial stationers. The number of analysis columns will depend on the amount of analysis you need.

Analysing the receipts

Usually, there are not as many types of receipts as payments, so not so much analysis is needed. For many small retail businesses, two columns are adequate – one for sales, and one for other receipts. Other businesses may have more types of receipts to analyse – the degree of analysis depends on how complex your business is. It may also depend on whether or not you are registered for VAT. Different types of sales may well suffer different rates of VAT. For instance, a typical village general store might analyse its sales between:

- food
- drinks – non alcoholic
- drinks – alcoholic
- stationery
- sweets and confectionery
- lottery tickets
- tobacco
- other goods.

There may be other ways of analysing sales – for example, between different geographical areas, including exports; between different salespersons; mail order businesses may want to analyse the response between different advertising sources. The way in which you analyse your receipts depends on:

- your type of business
- the information you want.

Always remember that it is *your* bookkeeping system, and it should apply *your* information needs. However, the more information you have, the better able you are to satisfy the demands of others, such as the Inland Revenue.

Figure 6 gives an example of a simple cash book receipts analysis.

Analysing the payments
Normally, there are more analysis headings for payments than for receipts. A basic outline often found is:

- direct business expenses (goods for resale, or for production of finished goods)
- indirect business expenses (overheads)
- purchase of assets (such as machinery or vehicles)
- money you take out of the business.

Within this general outline, there will be further analysis. You will certainly want to break down your overhead expenses further. The self assessment tax return requires your business expenses to be shown in a prescribed format (see Figure 7). You will therefore save yourself much work if you analyse your expenses in that way in your cash book.

Figure 8 gives an example of a simple cash book payments analysis.

Double entry bookkeeping
This is a method of complete bookkeeping. It was devised

RECEIPTS ANALYSIS

	DATE		DESCRIPTION	Amount	1 TYPE I SALES	2 TYPE 2 SALES	3 LOTTERY TICKETS	4 OTHER RECEIPTS	5	6
1	1.3.	00	TAKINGS	165 10	100 50	38 60	26 00			
2	2.3.	00	TAKINGS	113 50	98 20	15 30				
3	3.3.	00	FROM PRIVATE BANK	200 00				200 00		
4	4.3.	00	TAKINGS	149 90	110 30	29 60	10 00			
5	4.3.	00	INSURANCE CLAIM	550 00				550 00		
6	5.3.	00	TAKINGS	181 60	126 40	40 20	15 00			
7										
			TOTALS	1360 10	435 40	123 10	51 00	750 00		
8										
9										

Fig. 6. Cash book receipts analysis.

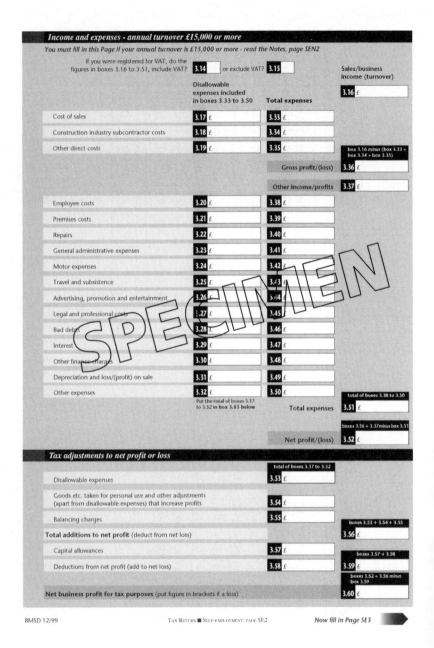

Fig. 7. Self-employment page of tax return.

PAYMENTS ANALYSIS

	DATE	DESCRIPTION	1 AMOUNT	2 RESALE GOODS	3 OVERHEADS	4 ASSETS	5 PRIVATE	6
1	1.3.00	A.B.C. LTD	120 00	120 00				
2	3.3.00	RATES	50 50		50 50			
3	3.3.00	CAR PURCHASED	1,500 00			1500 00		
4	4.3.00	OWN DRAWINGS	100 00				100 00	
5	5.3.00	X.Y.Z. LTD	150 60	150 60				
6	5.3.00	CAR INSURANCE	200 00		200 00			
7								
8		TOTALS	2,121 10	270 60	250 50	1,500 00	100 00	
9								

Fig. 8. Cash book payments analysis.

131

over 300 years ago by a monk, and is still used as the basis of all bookkeeping – even computerised systems use this method.

As the name suggests, each transaction is entered twice. One entry is in the account which 'gives', the other entry in the account which 'receives'. Imagine, for example, that you receive cash for goods that you have sold. The account that 'gives' is the sales, and the entry in the 'giving' account is called a credit. The account which 'receives' is the cash account (you have received cash). The entry in the receiving account is called a debit.

To distinguish debits from credits, they are written on opposite sides of the page. The accepted convention is that debits are on the left and credits on the right. Some accounts can have both debits and credits. The cash account, for example, is debited with receipts, and credited with payments.

At the end of the accounting period, all the accounts are balanced off – that is, the credits and the debits are added up, and the difference represents the balance of that account. All the balances on the accounts are then put together to make a trial balance. The total of all the debit balances must equal the total of all the credit balances, since each entry has been made twice, once on the debit and once on the credit side.

There are usually classes in double entry bookkeeping at night schools, and there are many books on the subject, some of them in the 'How To' series.

Other bookkeeping records
Between the simple cash book type of bookkeeping, and
the full double entry system, there are other bookkeeping
records which can be kept, and many businesses manage
with the simplest, or some form of intermediate records.

Sales day book
If you make sales on credit, you should keep a sales day
book and a sales ledger. A sales day book details all sales
made, preferably in date order, and in numerical order of
your sales invoices. A basic minimum would be six
columns, showing:

1. date
2. invoice number
3. name of customer
4. amount of goods or services
5. amount of VAT
6. total amount (i.e. 4 plus 5).

If you need to analyse your sales any further, you can add
further analysis columns. The columns are totalled
regularly – this is usually monthly. The totals represent
your sales for that period, whether you have been paid for
them or not.

If you are registered for VAT, you must pay over the VAT
on the sales, whether they are paid or not (unless you opt
for the special 'cash basis' scheme). By the same token,
you can also reclaim VAT on your purchases and expenses,
even before you have paid them.

Quite apart from the VAT aspect, what you want to know about your business is what your actual sales are. That tells you about your business turnover. The question of whether they are paid or not is another issue, related to how you control your debtors. You must be able to look at these two issues separately to manage your business properly.

Sales ledger

The sales ledger is the place where you record what each customer owes you. This is done by entering the sales to that customer as a debit in his own account, and then the money he pays you is entered as a credit. Usually there will be a debit balance on these accounts, since the customer will have bought goods or services from you, and then pay you for them later.

At any time, the balances on the ledger (i.e. the summary of all the individual accounts) can be totalled, and this tells you how much you are owed by customers. The balances can be further analysed according to how old they are, and an analysed list would show which customers were taking too long to pay.

Purchase day book

This works in the same way as a sales day book, but it is for the invoices you receive from suppliers and other creditors. This would also need a minimum of six columns:

1. date
2. invoice number

3. name of supplier
4. amount of goods or service
5. amount of VAT
6. total amount (i.e. 4 plus 5).

You will doubtless want to analyse your purchase invoices, so you can use as many analysis columns as you need. Once again, do not forget the analysis of expenses required by the Inland Revenue on your self assessment tax return.

Again, the book will be totalled by regular intervals – probably monthly – and you will be able to see how your different expenses are building up. The totals will also be used as the basis of your VAT claim for inputs tax each quarter.

Before you enter invoices in the purchase book, check them, to ensure that:

♦ they represent goods or services you have ordered
♦ they represent goods or services you have actually received
♦ the prices charged are what you agreed with the supplier
♦ the quantities are correct
♦ the calculations are correct.

Purchases ledger
Each item in the day book will be entered in an account for each supplier in the purchases ledger.

The invoices are entered as credits, and when you pay them, the payments are entered as debits. Normally, accounts in the purchase ledger will show a credit balance, since you will normally owe money to your suppliers.

At regular intervals, usually monthly, total each account to see what you owe them. You can then make the payment due, unless there is any particular problem or dispute. If the supplier offers a discount for prompt payment, make sure you pay within the time allowed for the discount to be taken.

Wages book

If you employ anybody, you need a wages book. This shows for each employee:

- the gross wage for each pay period (usually weekly or monthly)
- the deduction for tax
- the deduction for National Insurance
- any other deductions
- the net amount payable
- the employer's contribution to National Insurance.

You will also have a PAYE system from the Inland Revenue. This allows you to calculate the amount to pay over to the Inland Revenue for the tax and national insurance you have deducted from employees, and the employer's national insurance contribution.

Nominal ledger

This is the completion of the full double entry system of bookkeeping. There are accounts for all the types of income and expenditure, assets and liabilities. As well as the entries from the day books, the cash book and the petty cash book, there may also be journal entries, into the accounts of the nominal ledger. These are 'book entries' only, and transfer notional amounts from one account to another account. The journal entries cover such things as depreciation written off fixed assets.

All the ledger accounts are periodically totalled to produce a trial balance. If everything has been entered correctly, all the debit balances should equal all the credit balances.

Profit and loss account and balance sheet

All the balances in the trial balance can then be allocated to either the profit and loss account or the balance sheet. The profit and loss account contains all the items of income and expenses, and comparing these will show if you have made a profit or loss.

The balance sheet contains all the other items, which include assets and liabilities, and your private monies taken out of or put into the business. The balance sheet shows your position at the date of the balance sheet – you will have either net assets or net liabilities.

The profit and loss account and balance sheet are prepared at regular intervals. The interval depends on how regularly you need to keep track of your business. The accounts are usually made up at least yearly, and the Inland Revenue would expect regular annual accounts. There are detailed tax rules about the accounting dates used, and how frequently you can change the accounting dates.

Covering all the angles

There are many angles in running your business which must be accounted for in your bookkeeping. They are not necessarily the subject of a cash or cheque transaction, or an invoice. They can sometimes therefore be overlooked. Here are some of the things you must think about and account for.

Taking goods for your own or your family's use

If you take any business goods for private use, you must account fully for these items, both for income tax and for VAT purposes. It is best to pay for these at their full sales value. Otherwise, make sure that you add them to your sales, and work out the VAT due on them.

Supplying goods for business purposes

If you take goods from your trading stock to use for your own business, they should be added to your sales. However, they can also be deducted as a business expense. An example of this might be a publican who provides drinks or refreshments to a darts or skittles team.

Exchanging

You may supply goods or services to another person in exchange for other goods or services from them. No money changes hands, but clearly a commercial transaction has taken place. Your supply of goods or services must be valued and added to your sales. The goods or services for which you exchanged them may be a business expense, or they may be a private expense.

Private use

Some assets are used partly for business use and partly for private use. You should keep adequate records to enable you to charge the correct proportion as a business expense. The most obvious example is the use of a car. Keep a notebook or some other record in the car to record business mileage and private mileage. The total car expenses can then be divided between business and private use. The telephone is another example, and these are the sort of items that the Inland Revenue will look at if they examine your tax return.

Private accommodation

If you live on the same premises as the business, the expenses of the property should be split between business and private use. If necessary, you can get things such as water, gas and electricity metered separately. Council tax is levied on domestic accommodation, and business rates on business accommodation.

Paying expenses for the business

You may often find that you pay expenses for the business out of your own pocket, or even out of your own private bank account or building society account. Make sure that you reimburse yourself for these items from the business. If you are not able to do that, make sure that they are brought into the business accounts as a business expense.

Stocktaking

Keep records for your stock-take. This is usually carried out annually, but can be done more regularly. The stock of finished goods, raw materials and other items such as stationery must always be valued at the lower of its cost or its present market value.

Adjustments

For tax purposes, the law says that your accounts should be prepared on the accruals basis. This means that all income and expenses must be matched to the right accounting year. This may seem obvious, but some payments are not made exactly in the year to which they relate. For example, insurance is paid for a year in advance. So, if you paid your insurance premium on 1 March, and your year end is on 31 March, eleven months of that premium really relates to the next year.

Similarly, some expenses, such as electricity, are paid quarterly in arrears. Therefore, if your year end is on 31 March, and your meter was read on that day, you will not get the bill until some time in April, and the bill for the last three months' electricity of the year will not be paid until the next accounting year.

You must therefore adjust for all income and expenses of this type which are not paid in the year to which they relate. Making adjustments at the beginning and end of each year does this. These are known as prepayments (or payments in advance) and creditors (or accruals).

Keeping a computerised system

As more people become computer literate, computerised bookkeeping systems are becoming more popular. With personal financial programs, they are amongst the best selling software products.

There is a wide range of products to choose from, so you should have no trouble finding a system to suit you.

Among the front runners are:

- Pegasus
- Sage
- TAS Books
- Quick Books
- Page.

However, just as a desktop publisher does not transform you into a graphic designer, an accounting system in itself does not turn you into an accountant. If you already have an accountant, talk to him or her about the system before you buy it. If you want to go it alone, then ask yourself these questions about any system you look at:

1. Does it produce a balanced set of figures automatically?
2. Does it work on double entry principles?
3. Does it produce a detailed audit trail?
4. Does it allow you to tailor the analysis of income and expenses?
5. Does it show you what you owe to suppliers, and what your customers owe to you?
6. How easy is it to use? (Always try a demonstration.)

If the system covers all these areas, it goes a long way to providing what you need.

Writing up the books

Whether you have a computerised system or manual, you must discipline yourself to do the job regularly and accurately. If the records are not accurate, then the best system in the world is not worth much.

Don't put it off!

One of the best ways of ensuring that your records are as accurate as they can be is to write them up regularly and frequently. If you do not have to remember too far back, the chances are your work will be much more reliable.

If your business is not big enough to employ a book-keeper, then writing up the books is one of the chores that often gets left 'until a later time'. That 'later time' can get put back even further if an unexpected crisis occurs, or if you just feel too tired. You are then faced with a mammoth task which in itself is daunting. This can lead to rushing the job, or not giving it the attention it needs. That is when mistakes most easily occur.

Put aside a regular time to write up your books. If you cannot manage a time every day, find the time once or twice a week. Make it a regular spot in your diary, and you will get into a routine. You will find that doing the job regularly and frequently means that it is cut down into manageable chunks.

Try, if possible, to be away from the phone – if there is someone who can look after the business during your 'bookkeeping' time that minimises distractions. With a one man band, often the bookkeeping and administrative duties are done at home in the evenings.

ADMINISTRATION

Apart from the bookkeeping, there are other adminis-trative jobs to do. Letters have to be written, invoices typed or written, customers and suppliers chased. Once again, if you cannot afford a secretary, you must do these jobs yourself.

Try to do all your administrative duties together with the bookkeeping. Don't make your administration any more complicated than necessary. All you need is a simple system to enable you to keep on top of your work.

FILING

This is a vital part of the bookkeeping and administrative work. A good filing system is the key to all administrative work. Only you can work out the best system for yourself. Again, the best advice is to keep it simple. As long as you can lay your hand on something quickly, that is all that you need.

Once again, the golden rule is – Don't put it off!

RETAINING YOUR RECORDS

How long should you keep your business records? The main guidance here is in the tax laws. You must retain your accounting records for five years from the latest date for filing your tax return that includes those business accounts.

Example

Your business year end is 31 May. The accounts for the year ended 31 May 2004 will be included in your tax return for the year ended 5 April 2005. The latest date for filing that return is 31 January 2006. You must keep the records for a further five years, i.e. until 31 January 2011. However, if the Inspector of Taxes is making an enquiry into your tax return, you must keep the records until you have been notified that the enquiry has been completed. In exceptional circumstances, this could mean keeping the records longer than the five-year limit mentioned above.

You must therefore have enough space to keep all the records, and a way of identifying them for each year. Usually a box with a label is quite adequate, unless your business records are more bulky.

Penalties

If you do not produce adequate records when requested, or if you do not keep them the required period, the Inland Revenue can charge you penalties. They have indicated, however, that they will reserve the maximum penalty for cases which they suspect of being grossly fraudulent.

CHECKLIST

1. You need at least a cash book and a petty cash book.

2. Analyse your income and your expenses to suit yourself, but do not forget the tax requirements.

3. You may also keep a sales ledger, a purchase ledger, and a full double entry system.

4. Don't forget to cover all the angles.

5. You can get a computerised system, but ask for help and advice, unless you are sure of your ground.

6. Do all the administrative jobs regularly and frequently.

7. Keep your filing up to date.

8. Don't dispose of your records before it is safe to do so.

CASE STUDIES

Ralph finds an alternative

Ralph is a plumber. He does not have a full system of bookkeeping. He keeps an analysed cash book and petty cash book. Instead of keeping a full purchase ledger, he keeps all the invoices from his suppliers in a concertina file, arranged alphabetically.

When he pays his suppliers, he marks each invoice with the payment date, then transfers them to his main payments file, which is in date order, corresponding to the entries in the cash book.

He has a similar system for his customers. When he sends out an invoice, he keeps a copy in a concertina file, arranged alphabetically. When customers pay, he takes out the invoice, and writes on it the date it was paid. It is then filed with the 'received' items to correspond with the entries in the cash book.

Anthony keeps adequate accounts

Anthony runs a shoe shop, with no sales on credit. He likes to keep a record of sales of accessories, such as handbags, socks, tights, polishes and brushes. His till is able to give readings of sales under the two categories – shoes and accessories. It is also able to give a separate reading of children's shoes, which are zero rated for VAT.

He pays by cheque for the main suppliers and the main items of overheads. He keeps a petty cash tin, and pays small incidentals from that. He has a business bank account and a private bank account. He transfers from his business bank account to his private bank account a regular monthly allowance. He pays all his private expenses out of his private bank account. However, he pays his income tax and his pension premiums out of his business bank account.

Anthony's bookkeeping consists of:

- main cash book, showing receipts and expenses from the business bank account
- petty cash book
- stock-taking records
- records of goods taken from the shop for his own and family use
- mileage records for the car
- wages book for his part-time employee and his wife.

The cash book shows his analysis of different categories of sales, and any private money put into the business.

The payments side of the cash book analyses the payments between:

- purchases of goods for resale
- business expenses (with several columns for the analysis needed for the tax return)
- assets purchased
- private money taken from the business.

He keeps the following documents, which he files regularly:

- business bank account statements
- chequebook stubs

- paying-in book counterfoils
- invoices for cheque payments made
- till rolls for the sales
- petty cash vouchers.

Once the accounts have been finished, and the tax return sent off, he bundles up all the documents, puts them in a large box, labels it for the year, and puts it in his loft.

POINTS TO CONSIDER

1. What is the best time for you to put aside for the administrative duties?

2. How would you decide what degree of sophistication you need for your bookkeeping?

3. When would you reach the 'critical point' at which it would pay you to employ a bookkeeper or secretary?

4. Think about the information you need to run your business, and make the right decisions. What is the critical factor in your business – sales volume, sales mix, controlling costs, or something else? How could you tailor your bookkeeping system to enable you to get the information you need?

(12)

Insuring Your Risks

Insurance is one of those expenses which come around year after year, and you may be tempted to ask if you could not miss it out. You seem to pay in, and never make a claim.

> **Do not ask 'Can I afford to pay it?'**
> **Ask instead 'Can I afford not to pay it?'**

There are risks in all areas of business, and you could be wiped out if you did not have the right insurance cover. Some insurances are, indeed, compulsory. If you have employees, you are obliged to display an employer's liability insurance certificate. Certain types of business may be required to have particular types of cover under health, fire and safety regulations, and, of course, every road vehicle must carry at least third party insurance cover. If you have a mortgage on property, the mortgage company will almost certainly require at least fire and damage insurance cover on the building.

REVIEWING YOUR INSURANCES

Within this general guideline, always keep your insurances under review. It is probably not a good idea to change your insurance company every single year, to chase after the cheapest premiums. But it usually pays to have a thorough insurance review every five years. The best person to do this is an insurance broker whom you trust. The insurance industry is very sophisticated, and cover is available for every risk you could imagine, and a few you could never think of. So don't let yourself be talked into taking out every new insurance product that comes along.

Level of cover

An occasional review should focus on making sure you have the right level of cover. The level of cover is an extremely important factor. Under-insurance can be almost as devastating as not having any insurance cover at all. And sometimes you will find that the level of cover which was set some years ago is now excessive. The level of cover is particularly important in the following types of insurance:

- *Buildings* – insure for the rebuilding cost, which is not necessarily the same as the market value.

- *Stock* – make sure that you cover for the maximum amount of stock you could carry at any one time.

- *Business interruption* – the usual cover is for eighteen months' loss of profits based on your last annual profit figure.

- *Equipment and machinery* – make sure that you cover the cost of replacing machinery, which is not necessarily the same as its original cost.

Premiums

An insurance broker will be able to survey the market to check whether better premiums are available. Bear the following in mind when thinking about premiums:

- *Uninsured excess* – if you can accept a slightly higher level of excess (i.e. your claim is reduced by a fixed amount for each occurrence – for example, £50), you may be able to see a great reduction in your premium.

- *Discounts* – insurance companies often offer discounts on the premiums if you can show that you have taken precautionary measures to reduce the risk (for example, by fitting alarms or fire extinguisher sprinkling systems, etc.).

- *Frequency of premium* – you may be able to pay the premium quarterly or monthly instead of annually.

BUSINESS RISKS

There are packages of insurance cover available for practically all types of business. These insurances cover:

- damage and loss to business assets, including equipment and stock
- loss of profits (due to business interruption after a fire)
- specific risks in your trade or business.

Usually, these insurances will exclude certain things such as wear and tear, mechanical or electrical breakdown, shoplifting and pilfering. There may be cover available for these risks, but they will be the subject of a different policy.

Interruption insurance

This covers the loss which may follow a fire, due to disruption and damage to stock, equipment and records. Often, this will include loss of profits cover for terrorist action, denial of access to your property due to a fire in an adjacent building, loss of computer records, and loss of book debts.

The level of cover is based on a certain number of months' gross income, since it assumes that you will have to continue to pay fixed and overhead expenses, while your income is interrupted.

Credit insurance
This is insurance against debtors defaulting. It is often included in factoring and invoice discounting packages.

Directors and officers insurance
This covers claims or damages made against directors or other officers of a company on a breach of duty.

Employer's liability
This is a compulsory insurance. It covers claims made against an employer by an employee, for damages, injury, disease, etc. if negligence can be shown. The law states that cover should be for a minimum of £2 million.

Engineering insurance
This covers mechanical and electrical breakdown of machinery.

Fidelity insurance
This covers loss due to employees' dishonesty, theft or pilfering.

Fire insurance
This usually covers additional risks such as flood, storm

damage, impact by road vehicles or aeroplanes, subsidence, etc.

Key person insurance

This is cover for a key employee, whose death or absence would greatly affect the business. Insurance is available to cover the death or illness of a key person. This allows you to carry on the business by hiring a replacement during an absence caused by illness or until a permanent replacement can be found.

Plate glass insurance

Replacement can be costly, so it is worth taking out a special insurance if you have a shop front with a particularly big plate glass window.

Goods in transit insurance

This covers loss and damage to goods being transported to or from your premises, whether by your own transport or by a contracted carrier.

Legal expenses cover

If you become involved in a trade dispute, it is good to have insurance cover for legal expenses, so that you cannot be 'bluffed' into giving up a claim, or defending against what you believe to be a spurious claim.

Product liability

This covers claims against you arising from defective assembly, design, manufacture, repair and servicing of products. If you are the manufacturer, retailers may claim against you. If you are exporting, especially to the USA and Canada, make sure that you get extra cover.

Professional indemnity

Many professions, such as the law, accountancy, architecture and medicine, are subject to claims being made for negligence. Most of the professional bodies governing these professions make it a rule that the practitioner must obtain professional indemnity insurance as a prerequisite to being allowed to practise.

Public liability

This gives cover against claims from members of the public for negligence. This can be particularly important if:

◆ you have projecting signs in the street
◆ you do work on customers' premises
◆ you are in the construction industry.

But whatever business you are in, you should not neglect this insurance. Something as simple as a loose carpet could trigger a claim.

Travel insurance

The usual travel insurance cover is sometimes necessary if you or an employee has to travel a lot in the course of the business. Cover can be on the basis of single trips, or annual blanket cover. It will include such things as loss of baggage, medical expenses, ambulance cover, repatriation, hijack, delay, cancellation, etc.

Working from home

If you carry on your business from home, your ordinary private home insurance may not cover any loss or damage. Check this, and if necessary pay any extra premium.

CHECKLIST

1. Get help from an insurance broker you can trust.

2. Review your levels of cover and premiums regularly.

3. Cover the main areas of risk in your business.

CASE STUDIES

George is underinsured

George has a small engineering business. He has two men working for him, and he has been in business many years. He has a buildings fire insurance, a trade comprehensive insurance, and the compulsory insurances for employer's liability and road vehicles – a truck and a car. He does not have a mortgage on the premises, so he has not had reason to keep the insured amount under review.

He has not reviewed the insurances for many years. When he has a fire, he discovers to his dismay that he is grossly underinsured for the buildings fire insurance – rebuilding costs have escalated since he first insured, and the access is difficult, adding substantially to the rebuilding costs. In addition, his stock and work in progress is only insured for about half its real value, and the figures he used for the business interruption insurance are several years out of date.

As a consequence, he has to remortgage his house to get enough funds to rebuild, and to restock and re-equip the business.

POINTS TO CONSIDER

1. Do you know how to value your stock and equipment for fire insurance?

2. Are there any special risks inherent in your trade or business?

3. Can you take any precautions to reduce the risk, and get a discounted premium?

$$\binom{13}{}$$

Retiring

PROVIDING FOR YOUR RETIREMENT

You may only just have started working for yourself. So when do you start to think about retirement? The answer is – now!

It is never too early to start providing for your retirement. Any delay severely reduces the final benefit when you retire. As a self-employed person, you pay class 2 and class 4 National Insurance contributions. Class 2 contributions only qualify you for the basic state pension, and class 4 contributions do not get you any pension at all. They are simply an extra tax on the self-employed. Anyone who has tried to live on the basic state pension will tell you that it is not easy. So how can you start to provide for your retirement?

You can pay pension premiums into a personal pension scheme, and into the stakeholder pensions. Up to 1988 you could have paid into retirement annuity schemes. These ceased for new contributions in 1988, but if you had a scheme in force then, you can carry on contributing to it.

Personal pension schemes

The contributions to a personal pension scheme attract tax relief at your top marginal rate of tax. Because of the generous tax relief, there are certain restrictions.

Restrictions

The main function of a personal pension scheme must be to provide a retirement income. Therefore, you are precluded from taking benefits before the age of 50. There are, however, younger age limits agreed by the Inland Revenue for certain occupations. These include such things as downhill skiers, athletes or sportspersons, dancers, trapeze artists, divers, etc. You must take the benefit by age 75 at the latest.

The provision of life assurance is permitted as a secondary purpose of a personal pension scheme, but it must be subsidiary to the main purpose.

You may also take a percentage of the benefits in the form of a tax free lump sum when you retire and start taking benefits. This is limited to 25% of the fund in your personal pension scheme. The rest of the fund must be used to provide an annuity for the rest of your life (or the joint lives of you and your partner).

Limits of tax relief

Tax relief on the premiums is only given against relevant income. This includes self-employed earnings, employed earnings, and profits from furnished holiday lettings. If you do not have those types of income, you may pay into a personal pension scheme, but only up to £3,600 each year.

There is a limit on the contributions that qualify for tax relief. The limits depend on your age at the beginning of the tax year, and the amount of your net relevant earnings, as follows:

Age at the beginning of tax year	Percentage of net relevant earnings
up to 35	17.5%
36 to 45	20%
46 to 50	25%
51 to 55	30%
56 to 60	35%
61 or more	40%

There is an overall limit to the net relevant earnings figure on which the percentages are based. At the time of writing this is £99,000 of net relevant earnings.

Carry back of premiums
You may elect that premiums you pay in one tax year be 'carried back' to the previous year, and the premiums treated as if they were paid in that earlier year. This could be useful if:

◆ you could not afford to pay the premiums in one tax year, or
◆ you paid tax at a higher rate in the previous tax year, or
◆ rates of tax generally were higher in the previous year.

Choosing a policy
If you are looking for a personal pension scheme, there are a bewildering number of choices available, and a large number of salespersons, advertisements and web sites trying to sell them to you. A salesperson employed by the company will be earning their living by the commission they get from selling to you. Equally, an independent adviser will earn commission.

However, the fact that they earn commission from selling to you does not necessarily mean that you should not invest with them. You can still get good value from a pension scheme. Ask the following questions when choosing a scheme.

What is the basis of the fund growth?
Funds are usually unit linked or with profits. Unit linked means that the premiums you pay buy a certain number of units in a fund or funds provided by the company. Like unit trusts there are different types of funds – typical funds are managed, equity, property, geographical. The prices are quoted in the financial press, and the value of your pension fund at any time is the value of the units multiplied by the number of units you have. This means that the value of your fund can fluctuate.

With profits funds means that the investment profits each year are credited to your account with the company, and you share in the profits of the company as a whole. The profits are added each year by way of annual bonuses. Once given, these bonuses cannot be taken away. The idea is to smooth out the ups and downs of the investment market, so there will not be the sort of fluctuations you get in unit linked policies. Then, when the policy matures, there is also a terminal bonus, which is added to the value of the fund.

This makes you a member of the company. If the company is a mutual company, it could give you a windfall payout if the company were taken over or if it were demutualised.

What is the charging structure?

Many companies pay commission, and particularly in the case of regular premium policies, there is a large deduction from your fund in the first year or two. It could then take a few years for your fund to recuperate this deduction. This is known as 'front end loading'. In turn, this of course means that you will lose out if you cancel or suspend the policy in the early years.

How flexible is the policy?

Do you want to pay regular premiums, or a single premium? Does your policy give you the opportunity to suspend premiums if necessary? If you are paying regular monthly or yearly premiums, can you add on single premiums at a later date?

What is the death benefit if you die before taking the benefits?

Some policies would refund you the premiums, with or without interest, if you should die before taking the benefits. However, it is usually much better to have a policy which would pay out the value of the fund.

Taking the benefits

When the time comes to take the retirement benefits from your personal pension scheme, you have several options. The basic set up is that your contributions over the years have created a fund. You then use that fund to provide an annuity for the rest of your life. You must be careful about choosing the annuity you take. Once you have started it, you cannot change it.

Open market option

You do not have to take the annuity from the same company to which you have been contributing. You have the right to take the fund and use it to provide an annuity from any other company. It is therefore worthwhile looking at the annuity rates on offer before you take your benefits. Your company may, however, quote you one figure for the fund if you take their own annuity benefits, and a lower figure if you want to transfer the fund to another provider.

Tax free lump sum

As we have seen, you can take up to 25% of the fund as a tax free lump sum. The figures are slightly different for retirement annuity policies. It is usually better to take the lump sum. You can invest it to get an income, and you then have the capital to use or to pass on to your dependants. The annuity is an income for the rest of your life (or the joint lives of you and your partner), and when you die, the fund is lost.

You must use at least 75% of the fund to provide this annuity, but it is better to have 25% of the fund as capital that you can use.

Increasing annuity

The annuity rate quoted for your fund will be a 'flat rate' figure. That is to say, once it is fixed the amount of the annuity stays the same for the rest of your life.

You can, however, decide on an increasing annuity. This means that the amount of the annuity will increase each year. This increase can be a fixed amount (say, 3%) or tied to the official rate of inflation. Obviously, if you choose an increasing annuity, the starting point will be much lower. The choice can be something of a lottery. If you live longer, then an increasing annuity 'wins'. But if you die soon after taking the annuity, the fixed amount 'wins'.

With profits annuity

A recent refinement of the increasing annuity is the 'with profit' annuity. The fund continues to grow by investment gains, and the amount of the annuity increases every year in line with the profits. The performance of the with profits fund in which your annuity is invested will determine the amount by which your annuity grows – so it is likely that the growth will not be steady.

Unit linked annuity

This is slightly more risky than the with profits annuity. Your fund is invested in a unit linked fund. The annual annuity is therefore liable to fluctuations, and can actually decrease as well as increasing.

Guaranteed

You can get the annuity guaranteed for a minimum period, usually five years. This guarantee means that if you should die before the end of the guarantee period, the annuity would be paid out for the rest of the guarantee period to your dependants.

Sole life or joint lives

You can elect to have the annuity paid out for the rest of your life, or for the joint lives of you and your partner. Again, this will obviously affect the amount of the starting figure. The amount of the annuity can also be varied – it could, for example, be the full amount of the annuity paid for the rest of your life, with a fraction (say one-half or two-thirds) paid to your surviving partner.

A joint annuity can also be for a fixed amount or an increasing amount.

Phased withdrawal

If you have a series of policies, or if the amount in the fund is large enough, you can achieve a phased withdrawal. This means that you can start taking some of the retirement benefits, and gradually phase in taking the rest, until you are drawing all the benefits. If you have a series, of say, ten policies, you could take out the benefits of one each year for ten years, to gradually build up to a full pension.

This is particularly useful if you want to phase in your retirement, by gradually reducing your involvement in the business. If you want to do this, the best way is to set up your personal pension scheme as a series of policies right from the start.

Income drawdown

This is another recent innovation. It was introduced when annuity rates were low, and taking annuity benefits meant that you were 'locked in' to those rates for the rest of your life. The drawdown facility means that you do not have to take the annuity, but you can draw down a certain amount of the fund, and use it as you wish.

By this means, you postpone taking the benefits, and you can take them at a time when annuity rates are better. However, you must take the benefits by the age of 75 at the latest.

Stakeholder pensions

This is a form of pension provision introduced in 2001. It is aimed broadly at people earning between £8,000 and £20,000 per year. However, these pensions are available to anybody. If you are employed, self-employed or even unemployed, you can still benefit from the tax relief.

SELLING YOUR BUSINESS

You may have mixed feelings about selling the business and retiring. Indeed some people find that they cannot face retiring, and so just go on, until they die 'in harness'.

But most people want to enjoy a rewarding retirement. Once you have built up your business, you have a valuable asset, which you can sell. It is often true that the goodwill of the business rests with you personally. You have built it up over a number of years. The contacts with your suppliers, competitors and, most of all, your customers, make goodwill very personal.

Despite all that, people realise that you have to retire, and most will go with your business successor.

Planning ahead

It is always good to plan as far ahead as you can. Make plans for your retirement at least ten years ahead. Decide whether you want to phase out your retirement, or make a clean break.

Very often, you may have a good idea of who you would like to take on the business when you retire. It may well be a member of your family – perhaps the next generation. It may be someone who has worked for you – you may even have trained the person to do the job.

Planning in advance gives you and your successor the chance to smooth out the problems that might otherwise arise. Working with the person who is taking over means that you are able to show them all the aspects of the job – the administration and bookkeeping as well as the technical side. You are also able to make sure they build up a good relationship with customers and suppliers.

Handling the negotiations

Even if you have known and worked with your successor for a long time, you must handle the negotiations for sale in a business-like manner. Get a solicitor to draw up the agreement for sale, and suggest to the other party that they get an independent solicitor to act for them.

You will have to negotiate a price for the business, how that is to be paid, what is included in the sale and what is not, and the terms of the handover. It is quite usual to have a clause restricting the seller of the business from setting up in competition within a certain time period and within a certain geographical area around the business (say, a five mile radius).

You will also have to be prepared to supply information, such as the business accounts for the last five years.

Advertising the business

It may be that you do not have a buyer ready to take over your business. If so, you will have to advertise it for sale. Some estate agents deal with business sales as well as property sales. There are also specialist business transfer agents who deal only in business sales. They will, of course, take a commission, but they can often get a better price, and have access to a larger base of people looking to buy a business. They will have specialist knowledge of the issues involved in selling a business.

Paying tax on the business sale

The sale of a business is a disposal of an asset for the purposes of capital gains tax. Taper relief was introduced in 1998, to replace retirement relief and indexation relief. It works by reducing the gain liable to tax by reference to the amount of time the asset has been held since 5 April 1998. The taper is more generous for business assets than for personal assets. The maximum time for taper relief is ten years. The table below shows how this relief works for business assets.

Number of whole years asset is held	Percentage of gain chargeable to tax
Less than 1	100%
1	50%
2 or more	25%

This scale is in force from 6 April 2002.

Thus, the taper relief can never cover the whole of the gain – the most it will reduce it by is 75%.

PASSING THE BUSINESS ON TO YOUR FAMILY

You might want to pass on the business to the next generation of your family. The best advice is to start preparing for this as soon as possible. First of all, make sure that the next generation actually wants to take on the business. There have been many family arguments caused by a parent's unwarranted assumption that a child will want to take over the business.

If the child does want to do this, they should do all the training they can, and you should support them in it. It may mean some kind of vocational training, or university course. This could take them out of the business for several years. Be prepared for that.

Creating a partnership

One way of preparing the ground is to bring your child into partnership with you at a point when you feel they are ready for it. Their share of the profit can be determined, giving them an incentive to work for the benefit of the partnership business which will one day be theirs. That way, they learn the responsibilities of self-employment, and you can eventually pull out without too much disruption. It also makes a phased retirement easier. You can gradually reduce your involvement in the business, while also reducing your share of the profit.

There still remains the financial settlement, and you will no doubt have some capital in the business that your successor must make provision for paying out to you. It is still a good idea to have a solicitor to look at any agreements made, including drawing up the actual partnership agreement.

CHECKLIST

1. Start providing for your retirement as early as you can.

2. Choose the right pension policy for you.

3. Look at all the options when you take the benefits.

4. Plan ahead to sell your business.

5. Think about creating a partnership to ease the transition.

6. Get advice about all aspects of retiring.

CASE STUDIES

Fred retires in comfort

Fred started working for himself in his mid thirties. He had been a member of a company superannuation scheme, and his benefits under that scheme were frozen until he retired. As soon as he began self-employment, he started to contribute to a personal pension scheme. He made regular contributions, and with advice from an independent financial adviser, chose a scheme that allowed the increase of his regular premiums and the addition of lump sum premiums.

When he comes to retire at the age of 60, the funds have built up a substantial amount. The annuity rates are not good, so he chooses the drawdown scheme, and draws down 5% of the fund each year for three years. By this time the annuity rates have improved, so, with the advice of his adviser, he decides to take the benefits.

He chooses the open market option, and his financial adviser looks around the market to get the best annuity rate for the fund. This involves transferring the fund to another company, but that proves to be easy to do. He chooses a joint annuity for him and his wife, based on an annual 4% increase in the annuity. He also chooses to take 25% of the fund as a tax free lump sum. He invests this to produce an additional income for himself and his wife.

He has a good income, and can enjoy a comfortable retirement. In a couple of years' time, he will also receive the state pension.

POINTS TO CONSIDER

1. Can you afford to delay starting to provide for your retirement?

2. Will you need expert help in choosing a pension scheme?

3. Will you need expert help in deciding how to take the benefits?

4. Who do you want to take over the business when you retire?

Glossary

budget. A detailed plan of action translated into money terms.

business angel. A person who will provide finance and advice.

capital gains tax. A tax on profits made on selling assets.

County Court judgement. A legal means of enforcing a debt.

credit control. The process of controlling the money owed to you by debtors.

double entry. A form of bookkeeping giving complete records of all transactions.

factoring. A method of financing debts owing to you in business.

franchising. A method of carrying on business under licence from a nationally known company.

hire purchase. A means of financing an asset by instalment payments.

leasing. A means of financing an asset by temporary ownership, paying a rent.

limited company. A medium for carrying out business which distances the ownership from individuals.

marketing. Any action which makes selling easier or unnecessary.

National Insurance. A form of taxation to provide social security benefits.

overdraft. A form of borrowing from a bank, allowing your current account to overspend.

partnership. Relationship between individuals carrying on business together.

PAYE. A system of collecting tax and national insurance from employees and paying it over to the Inland Revenue.

personal pensions. A way of providing a pension for self-employed people.

secured loan. A loan tied to a charge on an asset.

stakeholder pensions. A type of government-sponsored pension scheme.

unsecured loan. A loan providing no security for the lender.

VAT. Value Added Tax – a tax on goods and services.

working capital. The money tied up in the day-to-day running of a business.

Further Reading

Bad Debts: Prevention and Cure, Donald B. Williams and Laurie Williams (Croner Publications)

Paying Less Tax, John Whiteley (How To Books)

Small Business Tax Guide, John Whiteley (How To Books)

Doing Business on the Internet, Graham Jones (How To Books)

Starting Your Own Business, Jim Green (How To Books)

Starting a Business from Home, Graham Jones (How To Books)

Working for Yourself, G. Golzen (Kogan Page)

Securing a Rewarding Retirement, Norman Toulson (How To Books)

Managing Your Time, Julie Amos (How To Books)

The Business Planner: A Complete Guide to Raising Finance, I. Maitland (Butterworth Heinemann)

Managing Your Business Accounts, Peter Taylor (How To Books)

Managing Budgets and Cash Flows, Peter Taylor (How To Books)

Everything is Negotiable: How to Negotiate and Win, Gavin Kennedy (Arrow Books)

Web Sites

GOVERNMENT BODIES

Business Link   www.businesslink.org
This is an official government body, but the web site is packed full of useful tips, information, links and advice. One of the most useful of all government sites for the self-employed.

Companies House   www.companies-house.gov.uk
This is the central registration agency for all limited companies.

Customs and Excise   www.hmce.gov.uk
This is the site of Customs and Excise, which administers VAT. A whole section of the site is devoted to VAT matters.

Department of Trade and Industry   www.dti.gov.uk
This is the government department dealing with all matters relating to trade and industry. It is more relevant to bigger businesses, but you may find some parts of the site useful.

Department of Work and Pensions   www.dwp.gov.uk
This is the department dealing with work, family and pensions. Contributions for Social Security are now dealt with by the Inland Revenue.

Inland Revenue   www.inlandrevenue.gov.uk
This site is very useful, and gives a lot of helpful advice for
the self-employed, as well as general tax advice.

Office of Fair Trading   www.oft.gov.uk
This is the site of the Office of Fair Trading, dealing with
all aspects of consumer regulation and law. Its slogan is
'Protecting customers; encouraging competition'.

OTHER OFFICIAL AND SEMI-OFFICIAL BODIES
Advertising Standards Authority   www.asa.org.uk
This body is the watchdog for advertising complaints.

Association of British Insurers   www.abi.org
This is the body representing British insurance companies.

Association of Chartered Certified Accountants
                                    www.acca.co.uk
This is the site of the body governing certified accountants, and can put you in touch with them.

British Chambers of Commerce
                            www.britishchambers.org.uk
This body co-ordinates the work of the many local
chambers of commerce and trade, which bring together
businesses in local areas to represent them in matters of
local importance – such as rating problems, and fighting
business crime.

British Franchise Association

www.british-franchise.org.uk
This is the body for franchising operations of all sorts.

Federation of Small Businsesses www.fsb.org.uk
This independent body champions the cause of small businesses. It is the UK's largest small business lobby group. The site gives advice and help on all sorts of matters, including things like dealing with late payers.

Institutes of Chartered Accountants

www.chartered-accountants.co.uk
This site covers the Institutes of England and Wales, Scotland and Ireland. It can put you in touch with chartered accountants anywhere in these regions.

National Federation of Enterprise Agencies

www.nfea.com
This is the national organisation of Enterprise Agencies.

Telework Association www.tca.org.uk
This is Europe's largest network association for tele-workers. The web site gives information about all aspects of teleworking, including items about telecottages.

INDEPENDENT COMMERCIAL ORGANISATIONS
Better Business www.better-business.co.uk
This site is the web site of the business magazine of the same name. It gives information on many areas, including producing business plans.

Bizwise   www.bizwise.co.uk
This site offers a wide range of business advice at a subscription – at the time of writing, £15 per month, or £150 per year. You can also use this site to market your business on their register.

Business Incubator Network   www.ukbi.co.uk
An association of 'incubators' giving mentoring and other help to new businesses.

Desk Demon   www.DeskDemon.co.uk
This site provides many free office tools, and a Royal Mail postcode search and telephone directory search.

Exchange and Mart   www.exchangeandmart.co.uk
This is the famous source of second-hand goods. It has a business section for all kinds of business equipment and services.

OneLondon Business Angels Network   www.olban.co.uk
A source for business angels in the London area.

Markets Unlocked   www.MarketsUnlocked.com
This is a UK-based market place for buying and selling. It claims to deal with everything your company buys, everything your company sells, in every industry sector, in every country.

National Business Angels Network   www.nban.com
The national organisation for business angels.

Startups   www.startups.co.uk
This site gives advice over a wide range of subjects, from
starting-up, franchising, through to business structure,
the law, business equipment, working at home, and much
more.

Virginbiz   www.virginbiz.net
Another good site with lots of advice. This one also
pushes many of its own products.

Working From Home   www.wfh.co.uk
This site is a British Telecom site, for those working from
home. It gives a link to other people working from home.
It provides a forum, links to useful sites, and business tips.

Index